CULTURES OF THE WORLD®

LIBYA

Peter Malcolm/Elie Losleben

BENCHMARK BOOKS

MARSHALL CAVENDISH
NEW YORK

PRECEDING PAGE
A Libyan family visits the Roman ruins at Leptis Magna.

Marshall Cavendish
99 White Plains Road
Tarrytown, NY 10591
Website: www.marshallcavendish.us

© Times Editions Pte Ltd 1996, 1993
© Marshall Cavendish International (Asia) Private Limited 2004
All rights reserved. First edition 1993. Second edition 2004.

® "Cultures of the World" is a registered trademark of Marshall Cavendish Corporation.

Originated and designed by Times Books International
An imprint of Marshall Cavendish International (Asia) Private Limited
A member of the Times Publishing Group

Library of Congress Cataloging-in-Publication Data
Malcolm, Peter, 1937-
Libya / by Peter Malcolm, Elizabeth Losleben.— 2nd ed.
   p. cm. — (Cultures of the world)
Includes bibliographical references and index.
Contents: Geography — History — Government — Economy — Environment — Libyans
minority — Lifestyle — Religion — Language — Arts — Leisure — Festivals — Food.
ISBN 0-7614-1702-8
1. Libya—Juvenile literature. [1. Libya.] I. Losleben, Elizabeth. II. Title. III. Series.
DT215.M3 2003
961.2—dc22   2003020887

Printed in China

7 6 5 4 3 2

CONTENTS

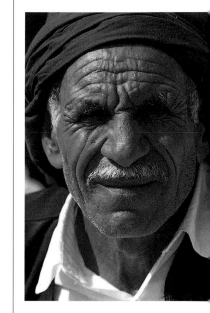

An old Libyan.

**One of the Roman ruins
in Libya.**

INTRODUCTION

LIBYA IS A COUNTRY of immense natural and cultural wealth. Bedouin and Tuareg nomads live in the south, where rich oil reserves lie deep beneath the sand. Berber communities live in villages and cities. Most of them are descendants of Berbers who married Arabs more than 1,000 years ago. Libya's vast oil wealth does not make up for its poor food production, however, and the economy remains heavily dependent on imports.

In the 20th century, Libya suffered a long period of political repression. Italian colonialism dominated the country from 1911 to 1951. Libya's first monarch reigned for 18 years before he was overthrown by a military coup that placed Colonel Muammar Qadhafi in power. Qadhafi remains the leader of Libya, and his notorious rule has made Libya the black sheep of international politics for years. His support of terrorist activities forced the United Nations to impose sanctions on Libya in 1992. UN sanctions were suspended in 1999, and life for Libyans began to improve.

GEOGRAPHY

LIBYA IS LOCATED IN THE CENTER of the northern coast of the African continent. Tunisia and Algeria lie to the west, Niger and Chad to the south, and Egypt and Sudan to the east. Libya's 679,362 square miles (1,759,547 square km) make it the fourth largest country in Africa, one-fifth the size of the United States and slightly larger than Alaska. Yet over 90 percent of it is desert, with rain falling only once every two or three years.

Over two-thirds of Libyans live on two narrow coastal strips near the Mediterranean Sea. Farther south, there are scattered oasis settlements in the desert—a bare, dry world of sand and rock interrupted in places by pipelines. When the stretches of desert are included, Libya's average population density is only five people per square mile (three people per square km).

Libyans of the desert have developed a way of life that allows them to survive in a harsh world. Their most precious possessions are animals—camels, sheep, and goats—and their survival depends on the availability of water.

Families adopt a nomadic lifestyle, constantly on the move to find water holes and fresh grazing land for their herds. Unfortunately, the unpredictable nature of the desert means that a water hole might be overflowing one season and dry the next, so families never settle anywhere permanently.

Opposite: **One of the many oases in Libya.**

Below: **A beach near Sabrata.**

THREE MAIN AREAS

Libya has three main regions: Tripolitania, Cyrenaica, and Fezzan. Until 1963, these regional names were the official names of provinces, but now they just indicate general geographic areas.

Tripolitania is Greek for "land of the three cities," in reference to Sabrata, Leptis Magna, and Oea (Tripoli). Its size is 110,000 square miles (284,900 square km), and it has a low, sandy coast occasionally fringed by lagoons. On the coastal Al-Jifarah Plain are salty marshes, sand dunes, and stretches of coarse grass, where wheat and barley are planted between rocky olive groves, together with fruit, cauliflower, tomatoes, and almonds.

The city of Tripoli has been the capital of Libya since its independence in 1951. It is also the country's main port and houses a third of Libya's total population. It is a fast-growing city, with new high-rise apartment buildings steadily taking the place of single-floor dwellings and improvised shanties. Palm trees and ornamental gardens fringe the Mediterranean shore, but any untended ground is hard and dusty.

Behind the coastal area, the land rises in a series of steps to the limestone ridge of Jabal Nafusah, which reaches a height of 2,500 feet (762 m) in some places. Old craters and lava rocks indicate its volcanic origin. On the southern slopes, some figs and barley are grown, but the countryside is too dry to support much life.

On the bare, red sandstone plateau of Al Hamra' in northwestern Libya, desert nomads graze small herds of sheep and goats. In some places attempts have been made to "pin down" the drifting sand with squared patterns of tough, rooted grass, and to plant species of fodder shrubs that can survive in dry areas.

The city of Tripoli.

8

To the east of this region are the Black Mountains, an unwielding wilderness of sharp, black basalt rock.

Cyrenaica (350,000 square miles, or 906,500 square km), Libya's other fertile coastal strip, has the towns of Banghazi and Tobruk. This area was once Greek, and the ruins of ancient Cyrene still attract visitors.

Inland, the limestone plateau of the Green Mountains (Jabal Akhdar) reaches a height of 3,000 feet (914 m) in two slender strips, each only a few miles wide. In season, the mountains are covered with a carpet of lilies, anemones, cyclamen, and narcissus. The higher parts have thick, thorny scrub, and there are patchy remains of juniper forests. Lotus grows in some of the damper southern valleys.

Tripoli continues to expand to accommodate the huge number of people who live in or commute into the city.

THE LIBYAN DESERT

To the south of the Green Mountains lie the sweeping sand dunes and stony plateaus of the Libyan Desert. This arid region extends as far as southwestern Egypt and northwestern Sudan. Little can survive on these windswept, sunbaked plains of gravel. The temperature is seldom below 40°F (4°C) and frequently over 100°F (38°C).

There are scattered settlements, mostly oases with a few thousand inhabitants. Stores of underground water have been discovered at Al-Kufrah, allowing agriculture to begin to flourish.

Desert scenery at Hatya Cemetery in Fezzan.

The bulk of the southern part of Libya is loosely known as Fezzan (270,270 square miles, or 700,000 square km), although this name actually applies only to a depression about 300 miles (480 km) south of Tripoli. Located in Fezzan are two of the larger oasis settlements, Sabha and Murzuq. This is harsh desert country where life depends on springs and wells fed by underground water.

From rock paintings discovered in the Sahara, it is clear that the region was once fertile, with enough pasture for large herds. Fezzan saw many traders traveling between the Phoenician-Roman coast and the rich areas of central Africa. Today, occasional camel caravans still thread their way across wastelands of sand, from oasis to oasis, as they have done for centuries. One of the five ancient north-south routes goes through Sabha, where the path diverges to go southeast and southwest. A fort stands on a flat-topped hill some distance from Sabha. It once housed a French garrison but is now a police post. Most of Fezzan is flat, but a section of the Tibesti Mountains, mostly within Chad, rises on the border to 7,440 feet (2,267 m)—the highest point in Libya.

SAHARA DESERT

Not all desert is sand. In fact, sand dunes cover only about a quarter of the 3.5 million square miles (9 million square km) of the Sahara, the largest desert in the world. Much of the Sahara is covered by rock and gravel. Its highest parts are the Tassili N'ajjer in Algeria and the Tibesti Mountains, both touching the southern borders of Libya. Surrounding these mountains are plains of gravel formed partly from ancient river beds. Six thousand years ago, the Sahara was green. We know this from fossils found in the Sahara and from the Tassili cave paintings and engravings of antelopes, ostriches, elephants, and lions. The Sahara's ancient inhabitants progressed from hunting to herding. Later paintings show cattle, sheep, and goats. Perhaps, as is happening in other parts of Africa today, overgrazing followed by erosion started to transform the once-green land into desert. Diminishing rainfall accomplished the rest. Stretching from the Atlantic Ocean to the Red Sea, the Sahara contains mountains that stand over 11,000 feet (3,350 m) high; lost oases; forgotten cities; salt, iron, copper, and uranium mines; oil wells; and plains of multicolored rock, gravel, and sand.

CLIMATE

Most of the country has a desert climate, with an average annual rainfall of only 10 inches (25 cm), which falls intermittently between November and early May.

Around the cities of Tripoli and Banghazi, the rainfall may reach 14 inches (36 cm) a year, but the desert areas (94 percent of the country) receive less than 4 inches (10 cm).

The desert at Ras Al Ghoul near Ghadamis.

THE BREADBASKET OF ROME

The northern shores of Africa, including the Nile valley, were the grain-producing areas of the Roman empire. In Libya, over 200 Roman wells have been discovered. Once cleaned, they work as well as they did 2,000 years ago. The Roman settlers and farmers dammed up narrow dry valleys known as wadis to trap moisture. Aqueducts 70 to 100 miles (110 to 160 km) long were built to carry water to the public baths in the thriving coastal cities.

Sabha, the main town of Fezzan, has been called the driest town in the world. Even in areas close to the Mediterranean, the summers are viciously dry and hot. Average winter temperatures vary from 52 to 63°F (11 to 17°C). Summer temperatures range from a low of 82°F (28°C) to a high of 100°F (38°C) but can rise to around 120°F (49°C). A world record of 136.4°F (58°C) was recorded in 1922 at Al Aziziyah, only 50 miles (80 km) southwest of Tripoli.

There are areas in the Libyan Desert where children grow to the age of 10 or more without ever having experienced rain. Such areas are called the sand seas because there are no shrubs or stones, only sand. Sandstorms called *ghibli* (GIB-lee) sweep across the desert two or three times a year in what seems like a wall of wind and red sand up to 2,000 feet (610 m) high. The winds can raise the temperature by as much as 20°F (7°C) in a few hours, causing severe damage to crops. Along with the storms come a parching dryness and sand that clogs eyes, nose, and ears.

The winters can be bitterly cold and unpleasant. Frost—sometimes even sleet and snow—is common in the mountains, and the desert nights are chilling. The winter rains along the Gulf of Sirte coast can turn limestone dust from the surrounding desert into seas of mud that make travel slow or almost impossible.

The high inland ranges receive only an inch or two of light winter rain each year. This is enough for the scattered spiny shrubs to survive, providing grazing land for the hardy sheep and goats of many nomadic groups.

There are no permanent rivers anywhere in Libya. If a rainstorm does occur, the streams that flow downhill to the valleys are soon lost in the dry earth. Droughts that last one to two years occur every five or six years.

WHAT LIVES IN THIS LAND?

In this dry climate, grass grows where it can. Esparto grass was once Libya's main export crop. It was used for making fine paper and rope. Herbs grow near the sea, including the asphodel lily, which the Greeks associated with death and planted on graves. Wild pistachios and henna shrubs that make a deep-red dye grow in the oases. The dye is used by North African women to paint designs on their hands and to tint their hair.

The most common animals in Libya are domesticated, including sheep, goats, cattle, horses, camels, and donkeys. Where there is sufficient shade and water, one can also see hyenas, jackals, and wildcats.

In the dry desert areas lies a wilderness empty of life during the day. Most lizards, snakes, and rodents would die in a few minutes in the hot sun, so dune creatures have learned to burrow underground, where it is cooler.

When the sun goes down and the sand cools, animals such as the jerboa come out to feed. With a tail almost as long as its 6-inch (15-cm) body, the mouse-like jerboa moves in a series of jumps with its forefeet held together, small carnivores such as fennecs (small foxes) watching for them. Fennecs obtain the water they need by eating jerboas as well as lizards and beetles.

A small farm near Zuwarah.

Snakes and lizards are cold-blooded, meaning their blood temperature is not constant. At night, their body temperature falls so low that in the morning, they must bask in the sun in order to bring their bodies back into working condition. During that time, they are vulnerable to predators such as hawks and foxes. If they lie in the sun for too long, they overheat, so they soon dig their way underground for shelter.

The skink is a common desert lizard. It has a wedge-shaped jaw, handy for digging sheltering holes in loose sand, and its eyes are covered with transparent scales. It is sometimes called a sandfish because when it runs, it looks as if it is swimming through the sand.

Skinks are regarded as delicacies by the desert nomads, who gut and roast them on skewers. Skinks are small and easy to take care of, and children in towns sometimes keep them as pets.

Most of the desert gazelle have been hunted for food and skins, but there is one breed of antelope that can be found in small pockets in the Idhan Desert near the Algerian border. This is the lumbering addax antelope, which is highly endangered. It seems to survive without water. Nomads believe that the juice from the vegetable matter in the stomach of an addax can cure any illness, from scorpion bites to food poisoning.

Many types of reptiles, including lizards, can be found among the rocks of the Sahara Desert.

Workers building a giant reservoir at Suluq.

WHAT'S BEING DONE?

In ancient times, much of Libya was fertile. The Romans built elaborate irrigation systems, as the ruins of huge cisterns indicate. There were apparently abundant supplies of wheat, barley, citrus fruits, olives, and dates.

Libya's revolutionary leader Colonel Muammar Qadhafi once promised that "the desert will bloom." A three-year plan was launched in 1973, followed by a more ambitious five-year plan in 1976. The aim was to make fuller use of natural resources, increase agricultural production, and create self-sufficient communities in agricultural areas. Nevertheless, the country still imports 75 percent of its food.

In the coastal areas, small amounts of petroleum waste mixed with other products have been sprinkled on the surface of sand dunes to prevent wind erosion. This has allowed eucalyptus trees to take root on the dunes. Coarse grass has been planted in square grids to prevent the sand from drifting.

In 1984 construction began on a pipeline more than 1,000 miles (1,610 km) long. Known as the Great Man-Made River, it was designed to bring water to northern Libya from deep underground reserves in the Sahara. However, it has not increased food production dramatically.

THE PALM TREE

In Libya, palm trees are found either by the sea or by most oases. It is never too hot or cold for the date palm, which survives night frosts and even snow. Date palms are either male or female. Pollen from a male tree is necessary for a female tree to produce fruit. The Bedouin believe palms that grow close together are friends. If one dies, the other trees will droop in mourning.

Nomads use every part of the date palm. The trunk provides timber, fuel, and fiber to make sacks and rope; the stalks are used for fences and roofs; the stringy part of the leaf is woven into baskets, mats, and sandals; and the juice of the young palm makes a sweet drink that can be fermented into palm wine. And, of course, there is the fruit. Dates are the nomad's daily bread. Dried and ground, they provide date flour, while their juice makes date honey. Even the date stones are ground and mixed with fodder for cattle or roasted to produce date coffee, a very bitter drink.

FEATHERED FOWL

The birds of Libya include eagles, hawks, vultures, wagtails, owls, ravens, black and white wheatears, partridges, and sandgrouse. Sandgrouse have special water-absorbent feathers that allow them to carry moisture back to their nest to cool their eggs. The noble falcon is seldom seen flying wild, though there are desert sheikhs who keep trained falcons for hunting small game or other birds.

The desert lark has a special place in nomadic tradition. Children are warned not to follow it. If they follow the lark a yard or two, and then a few more, they may easily get lost in the desert.

A vulture in the Libyan Desert.

THE CAMEL

Although motorized transportation is common in Libya, the camel remains valuable for long journeys and is used for plowing. A camel's speed rarely exceeds 4 miles (6 km) an hour. It can be forced into a rapid trot, but only for a few minutes or it will go lame. Owners look after camels carefully because to own many camels is a sign of great wealth.

The camel can drink 20 gallons (90 l) of water at one time. But ignore rumors that this water is stored in its hump; the hump is made of fat and does not store water. The camel stores its main supply of liquid in its stomach, which has three sections and can hold over 50 gallons (225 l). When all that is used up, the camel goes on for two or three days on the liquid stored in its body tissues.

The camel is actually an Asiatic animal and was not introduced to the deserts west of the Nile River until the first century B.C. Known as the ship of the desert, the one-humped Arabian camel can survive on dry twigs and can smell water up to a mile away. It lives for 40 years or more, and can carry a load of 1,000 pounds (450 kg) and travel 25 miles (40 km) a day. The nomadic Libyans make use of every part of a camel carcass. Its thick hide is used to make sandals, and its hump provides lard. The meat of young camels is eaten and camel's milk is drunk and used to make cheese. Camel droppings are dried for fuel.

In Biblical times, when the Hebrew nation under Gideon fought the various peoples of Canaan, the raiding Midianites that attacked the Israelites rode on camels. The sight of the raiders on these animals—creatures previously considered wild and untameable—frightened the mighty Hebrew soldiers. Even trained camels can be haughty and vicious; they spit, bite and kick when they are annoyed.

HISTORY

FOR HUNDREDS OF YEARS, the name Libya referred to all of Africa except Egypt. To its Mediterranean shores came cautious visitors from different exploring nations. The oases in the interior and the few fertile areas were settled by Berber nomads some time before 2000 B.C.

From about 1000 B.C., Phoenician sailors from what is now known as Lebanon began to visit the North African coast in search of gold, silver, ivory, apes, and peacocks. They founded Carthage (in modern-day Tunisia), and Carthaginian ships and armies challenged the might of the Roman empire. By then, the Greeks had founded the city of Cyrene (in the Al Jabar Al Akhdar region of present-day Libya), one of the cultural centers of the Greco-Roman world. Cyrene was a place of learning, where doctors and philosophers thrived. Wine, wool, and medicinal herbs were produced there. In 67 B.C. Cyrenaica, together with Crete, became a province of the Roman Empire.

The Romans destroyed Carthage in 146 B.C. and gained control of North Africa. Libya was developed into a useful grain-producing area. The Romans built the fine cities of Sabrata, Leptis Magna, and Oea in what is now Tripolitania.

After A.D. 435 Tripolitania fell into the hands of the Vandals and Byzantine Greeks before the Arab conquest in 642.

Opposite: **Leptis Magna, an ancient Roman city in Libya, is now a World Heritage Site.**

Below: **Sabrata.**

BARBARIANS

Greeks and Romans called all foreigners barbarians, meaning babblers, as they spoke a language no Greek or Roman could understand. That is how the Berber people, living inland in the Sahara Desert and mountains, got their name. The Berbers, or Amazigh, controlled the caravan routes across Africa, using horse-drawn war chariots to terrify their foes. Although they paid taxes to Rome, they remained fiercely independent. A line of Roman-built forts, including Leptis Magna, built by Septimius Severus (*above*), protected the prosperous coastal cities. Even the Germanic Vandals, who broke up the Roman empire in 410 and swept through Spain and the northern shores of Africa, never subdued the Berbers.

THE ARRIVAL OF ISLAM

In the seventh century, Islamic armies from the Middle East swept westward until they controlled all of North Africa and half of Spain. They brought with them their religion and language. The Arabs were not town dwellers, and the Roman cities were left to the enveloping sand, apart from the central area of Oea, which was maintained as a fort and on which the city of Tripoli now stands. There is still debate as to whether Islamic armies offered the inhabitants the choice of conversion to their religion, although Islam states that no one should be forced to convert.

After the death of Muhammad, Islam's founder, rule over the Islamic conquests passed into the hands of the caliphs, Muhammad's successors. Libya became part of the area controlled by the legendary Haroun al-Raschid of Baghdad. He appointed a local governor to rule from what is now Kairouan in Tunisia. In the struggles for power between successive caliphs, Libya changed allegiance to Egypt and then back to Baghdad.

In 1051 the Arabs in Tunisia, Tripolitania, and Cyrenaica rebelled against the powerful Fatimid caliphs of Cairo. Not only did the Fatimids send armies to subdue these provinces, they also sent families and livestock to populate the area. This was the real Arab invasion of North Africa. The newcomers intermarried with the local people, and the Arabic language and way of life became a mainstay of Libyan culture.

For over 300 years, marauding fleets of pirates based in Tripoli made the North African coast feared by all who sailed the Mediterranean. They seized trading vessels in the Mediterranean, plundered the cargoes, and sold the crews into slavery. In Spain, where the Arab invaders had settled, Christian armies were gathering. In 1510 a European expedition captured Tripoli, and the Order of Knights of the Hospital of St. John of Jerusalem sent a detachment of soldiers from Malta to build a castle there.

Despite the success of Islamic armies in conquering North Africa, they had trouble defeating the Berbers, who were led by a chieftain named Kusaylah and later a woman named Kahinah. It took the Arabs 15 years to finally overcome Berber resistance.

23

INVASION OF EMPIRE BUILDERS

Turkish Muslims from the Ottoman empire invaded Libya in 1551. They captured Tripoli, encouraged pirate fleets to sail again, and even made expeditions against the Berbers inland. In 1799 the young United States of America began paying an annual tribute to the Turks to ensure safe passage for its ships. Turkish soldiers, called janissaries, also settled in Libya and married local women. Libya remained under Turkish influence for three centuries and buildings from the Turkish period still stand today.

The Tripoli Castle, built by Turks of the Ottoman empire.

In 1911 Italy declared war on Turkey and invaded Libya. Beneath the sand, the Italians found the impressive remains of cities built by their Roman ancestors. They felt they were returning to lands that had once been theirs. (Benito Mussolini was a newspaper editor at that time and strongly criticized the invasion. He was jailed for opposing the invasion. When he became the dictator of Fascist Italy, he counted Libya and Ethiopia as part of the "new empire.") There was a deliberate attempt by the Italian army to destroy Arab culture. Libyans in the occupied areas were given limited political rights, and those who refused to accept Italian authority were massacred.

Stories are still told of the Italian army's cruelty: how they sealed Bedouin wells, destroyed herds of cattle, drove people into concentration camps, and dropped resistance leaders from airplanes. The hanging of Libyans in every city became a daily event. Despite their unpopularity, more than 150,000 Italians settled in Libya.

THE SANUSI MOVEMENT

After making the pilgrimage to Mecca, a Berber leader named Sheikh Muhammad ibn Ali al-Sanusi decided that Islam needed strengthening against the persuasive attractions of the Western world. He opened a series of religious lodges. The first was in Mecca, and another in Libya. By 1867 there were 50 lodges in Cyrenaica. The aim of the Sanusi Muslims was to live pious lives and purify their faith. In due course, this brotherhood of stern-minded Arabs made highly effective warriors against the Italians.

The Sanusi (sahn-OO-see) sect became the backbone of Libyan resistance. This was the time of the legendary Sanusi hero, Umar al-Mukhtar, a simple country schoolteacher who led the Libyan resistance. Leading a force of nomadic fighters that rose to 6,000 people, Umar led intermittent attacks on Italian communications and supply lines for nearly 20 years. In September 1931 he was wounded and captured in the Green Mountains and subsequently hanged before a crowd of 20,000 sad Libyans. (His tomb is shown below.) During World War II, many Sanusis fled to Egypt and joined the Allied forces to continue the fight against the Italians.

The war cemetery at Tobruk, the Libyan port that was the site of one of the fiercest battles of World War II.

TWO WORLD WARS

World War I affected Libya only because Italy gained control of the country, but many World War II battles were fought across North Africa. The Desert War was a gigantic conflict that swept back and forth through Tunisia, Libya, and Egypt. Allied armies and Axis troops advanced and retreated as much as 4,000 miles (6,500 km). Britain's Eighth Army and Germany's Afrika Korps earned their fame as much from battling the Libyan Desert as from battling each other.

Much of the fighting revolved around the Libyan port of Tobruk. Long lines of gravestones in the desert form the military cemeteries of Allied and Axis troops. Even today, wandering camels and sometimes herdsmen are killed by one of the thousands of landmines that lie buried as deadly souvenirs of the Desert War.

After the war, the victorious Allied powers realized Libya's strategic importance and argued long about who should take over the land. But it seemed best to give Libya the chance to make its own choice. So in 1951 the United Nations declared Libya an independent state, and a national assembly chose Muhammad Idris al-Sanusi as its first monarch.

MONARCHY

King Idris swiftly showed the style of rule he favored—absolute. There was one hotly contested election in 1952, after which Idris banned all political parties, banished most of his relatives to the desert, and deported the leader of the main opposition party. Though improvements were soon made in Libyan education and health services, the people in power became richer, while the poor remained poor.

As the Western world powers had hoped, Idris welcomed British and U.S. military bases into Libya. Wheelus Air Force Base near Tripoli became a main training base for the North Atlantic Treaty Organization (NATO) and a part of the Western defense system. At the time of independence, Libya was poverty-stricken, and its people mostly illiterate. In return for the military bases, the United States and Britain provided substantial economic and technical aid.

One of the benefits of having foreign experts in Libya was the discovery of oil fields in the desert. By 1960 there were 35 oil wells in production. Exports of petroleum rose from 8 million tons in 1962 to over 70 million tons in 1966. Much of the profit went to the foreign countries that had done the drilling. Unfortunately, little of Libya's new-found wealth was passed to those who needed it.

As the king's health began to fail, corruption in his government increased. Many Libyans wished for a new government. Some had been planning for many years to organize a coup.

Muhammad Idris al-Sanusi, the first and only king of Libya.

THE REVOLUTION

In the early morning of September 1, 1969, while King Idris was on vacation in Turkey, Libyan army officers captured the state palace in Tripoli in a bloodless coup. A few hours later, the leader of the coup, Muammar Abu Minyar al-Qadhafi, seized a radio station in Banghazi and broadcast the news. He told listening Libyans that the monarchy had been replaced by a republic. Many Libyan army units had wanted to seize control for months, but Qadhafi's group acted first.

The king expected the United States or Britain to restore him to the throne. But neither nation wished to stir up trouble in the Middle East. Idris soon announced that he was passing the throne on to his son, Crown Prince Hassan al-Reda. The prince was promptly arrested and hastily agreed to urge Libyans to support the new regime. Idris went into exile in Egypt where he died in 1983.

In an interview with an Egyptian editor, Qadhafi expressed the hope that Egypt's president, Gamal Abdel Nasser, whom Qadhafi admired greatly, would take over the country. When that did not happen, Qadhafi promoted himself to colonel and was automatically accepted as chairman of the new government. At 27 he became the ruler of Libya. His main aims quickly became apparent: to build unity among the Arab countries, to create a Libyan socialist republic based on Islamic law, and to destroy Israel, which he regarded as the prime enemy of the Arab world.

THE LONE FALCON

Qadhafi was born to a family of desert nomads. His family were Berbers. As one of his grandfathers had been killed by the Italian invaders, and his father and uncle imprisoned for resisting them, young Qadhafi learned to hate Europeans at an early age.

By the age of 10, his teachers recognized that he was remarkably intelligent. He rose to the top of his class and was promoted swiftly. One of his early fascinations was the radio. He would listen to it for hours, often going without food so he could buy new batteries. The *Voice of the Arabs* programs broadcast from Egypt allowed Qadhafi to listen to President Nasser, who became his hero.

While attending high school in Sabha, Qadhafi began to recruit secret cells of students with the plan to overthrow the Libyan monarchy. The plan leaked and Qadhafi was expelled. Undaunted, he attended another school, graduated with honors, and entered the University of Libya. He continued planning to overthrow the king. After earning a degree in law, he joined the army and steadily recruited more followers. By August 1969, Qadhafi was acting adjutant of the Libyan Signal Corps. With most of Libya's 7,000-strong army already sympathetic to the revolutionary cause, he launched the coup on September 1, 1969.

"Qadhafi's leadership is a combination of revolutionary terror and his own personal qualities as a messianic leader."

—Comment in African Contemporary Record, 1987–88

THE FALCON'S FLIGHT

Four months after the coup, Qadhafi married a teacher at a midnight ceremony attended by Nasser. The marriage failed and they divorced after the birth of one son. In July 1970 Qadhafi married a nurse, who bore him more children.

Qadhafi created controversy in the Middle East and beyond. After Nasser died in 1970, his successor, Anwar Sadat, did not share Qadhafi's dream for Arab unity. This led to a deterioration in relations with Egypt. When Sadat tried to make peace with Israel, Qadhafi rallied several Arab states to freeze relations with Egypt. On the international stage, he astounded politicians and rulers with his lack of tact.

Obsessed with power and the desire for perfection in his country, Qadhafi instituted the death penalty for anyone who dared to engage in political activity against him. Strikes were forbidden. The Arab Socialist Union became Libya's only political party. To support his ideals, Qadhafi produced the *Green Book* in three volumes, setting out his theories for the perfect democracy, the perfect economy, and the way of life that he called the Third Universe Theory. He had three unshakable obsessions: revolution, Islam, and Arab unity.

In an effort to show that he was still a humble Berber at heart, Qadhafi declared his only title as Brother Colonel. He was photographed in his family tent wearing Arab robes, although his usual dress was an army uniform. He roamed the streets in disguise, sharing the talk of the Libyan people. Slightly built, with a deep, quiet voice and boyish grin, he walked with bent shoulders and hands in his pockets.

Today, Qadhafi is regarded with distrust by leaders of many nations, including the Arab nations he tried so hard to unite. Yet to his own people, he is the champion of the poor, the upholder of Islam, and the liberator from colonialism.

CULTURAL REVOLUTION

On April 15, 1973, the day on which Prophet Muhammad's birthday was being celebrated, the announcement of Libya's new Cultural Revolution was made. It was designed to uphold the ideals of the Al-Fatah revolution (in 1969 when Qadhafi came to power) and give the country to its people. It was also a further excuse to purge the country of any dissident elements. To expel communists and capitalists is one thing; to imprison thousands of peaceful Libyans who happen to disagree is another altogether.

Arabic was made the official language by a Revolutionary Committee firmly guided by Qadhafi. Anything printed in English or Italian was removed. Following strict Islamic law, alcohol, revealing clothes, bars, casinos, and unsuitable literature were banned. Hundreds of books were burned.

Nevertheless, the ordinary person in Libya found that the general quality of life began to improve. Roads, hospitals, and schools were built. Irrigation projects were planned to increase food production. The factories and assets of foreign companies were nationalized by the state. By 1977 Libya was the richest country on the African continent.

"We will teach how a people can take up arms to stage a revolution."

—Muammar Qadhafi

INTERNATIONAL TERRORISM

Certain that Libya had taken the right step toward freedom, Qadhafi began supporting other insurgent movements around the world. In the 1970s and 1980s Libyan wealth backed terrorists in Northern Ireland, the Palestine Liberation Organization, the Basque separatist movement in Spain, and South African black activists fighting apartheid. In 1979 Qadhafi sent troops to support the brutal dictator, Idi Amin, in Uganda. It is suspected that there may have been as many as 20 camps in Libya training over 7,000 terrorists for subversive activities around the world.

In 1988 Libya was believed to have been involved in the bombing of a commercial airplane in the skies over Lockerbie, Scotland, in which hundreds of people were killed. When Qadhafi refused to hand over the two Libyans suspected in the bombing, many countries severed diplomatic ties with Libya.

In 1992 the United Nations imposed sanctions on Libya for its continued harboring of the two suspects. In 1999 Qadhafi finally agreed to let the men stand trial in the Netherlands under Scottish law, and the UN sanctions were suspended. The trial came to an end in 2001, with one suspect jailed and another set free. In August 2003 Libya admitted responsibility for the Lockerbie incident and the United Nations agreed to lift sanctions. However, the United States continues to boycott relations with Libya.

FOREIGN POLICY

In the 1980s the prime targets of Qadhafi's aggression were Israel and South Africa—the first seen as anti-Arab, and the other anti-black.

When South Africa reverted to majority black rule, Libya renewed diplomatic relations with the country. However, Libya has rejected the Middle East peace process, and no Libyan is allowed to travel to Israel.

In March 1986, U.S. warships deliberately sailed into the Gulf of Sirte, which Qadhafi had claimed as Libyan waters. Libya instantly launched an attack that backfired—Libyan vessels were sunk or damaged. Days later, a series of terrorist attacks around the world seemed to implicate Libya. The United States launched an air attack on Tripoli and Banghazi, hoping to kill Qadhafi. They failed, but Qadhafi's adopted daughter was killed.

In recent times, Qadhafi has sought closer ties with African and Arab countries. The countries are cautious in their relations with Libya because they do not want to alienate Western powers.

Qadhafi is a strong supporter of African and Arab unity. He is visibly involved in the Organization of African Unity. However, his vision of a "United States of Africa" or his ideas about the merging of Israel and Palestine into a single country, "Israeltine," are rarely pursued or taken seriously by international leaders. Since the United Nations suspended sanctions on Libya in 1999, many countries, except the United States, have reestablished commercial and diplomatic ties.

A mural in Qadhafi's bombed house depicting the U.S. air raid that almost killed him.

GOVERNMENT

FROM ITS DAYS AS A COLLECTION of scattered towns and tribes dominated by the Ottoman empire and then the Italians, Libya became a modern nation that first gained an independent government in 1951. The rule of King Idris proved to be a dictatorship. He took all power into his own hands and banished those who offered any threat or opposition.

The new constitution approved by the United Nations in 1951 set up an elected house of representatives with 55 members and an upper house or senate, half of whom were nominated by the king. The king also had the power to appoint his own provincial governors, to veto legislation, and to dissolve the lower house completely if he so wished.

Within two years, all political parties were banned. Idris made no attempt to meet the desires of his people by changing Libya from a monarchy (rule by a king or queen) to a republic (rule by an elected president).

The king's unpopularity became the grounds for revolution. The coup in September 1969 left Idris in exile and put Qadhafi in power. A 12-man revolutionary council was appointed, with Qadhafi as chairman. Libya was proclaimed "an Arab democratic and free republic." Ethnic leaders soon lost much of their power, and traditional interior boundaries ceased to exist. There is now only one political party: the Arab Socialist Union, formed in 1971, that allows all Libyans to participate in the government through their local popular congresses.

In March 1977 the General People's Congress renamed the country the Socialist People's Libyan Arab Jamahiriya. (*Jamahiriya* is an Arabic word meaning republic.) With all power delegated to various committees, Libya claimed to be the first and only country in the world with "no government." People learned to talk of "the authorities" rather than "the government."

Opposite: **Libyan leader Muammar Qadhafi attends a meeting to discuss regional politics.**

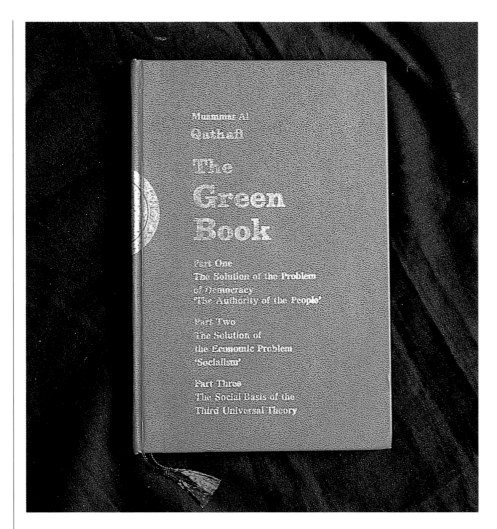

The *Green Book*.

THE GREAT GREEN BOOK

Between 1976 and 1979, Qadhafi produced his three-volume *Green Book*, outlining his "final solution to the problem of governing" in three points:

1. The solution to the problems of democracy is to give authority to the people. Democracy is not government; it is the formation of committees everywhere, and "supervision of the people by the people."

2. The solution to economic problems is socialism. People should be "partners, not wage workers." They should control the places where they work and own homes.

SOME SAYINGS OF QADHAFI:

"Racism, barbarism, and savagery are deep-rooted in the ethics of the Western imperialist colonialists … They are determined that African unity will not be established."

"All the efforts [of the Organization of African Unity] should be directed to the liberation of Palestine and South Africa, and the destruction of the racist regimes."

"We have given training to thousands of Africans—on Libyan soil—who took part in the liberation of a number of African countries."

3. The solution to social problems is the Third Universe Theory. This emphasizes the importance of family and tribal unity, the role of women (slightly inferior to men, and primarily to marry, and bear and raise children), the protection of minorities, and "how the blacks will prevail in the world."

According to Qadhafi, these theories were intended to steer Libya away from the evils of Western-style democracy with its free-market capitalism and Marxist communism with its all-powerful politburo.

THE LAW

While the country is run by the General People's Congress (a body of some 1,000 members formed from elected and appointed bodies), everyday life in Libya is ruled by strict Islamic law.

The sacred law of Islam is called *Shari'ah* (SHARI-ya), which means the path of Allah's commandments. Allah is the Arabic word for God. *Shari'ah* is sometimes summarized as:

- what God has commanded
- what God has recommended
- what God has left for us to choose
- what God disapproves of
- what God has forbidden

The *Shari'ah* courts deal with family matters and business and property claims. Islamic law, if fully enforced, threatens such punishments as the amputation of a thief's hands.

There is also a criminal code of justice in Libya based mainly on the Egyptian model that has judges and a court of appeal. But all family matters are settled according to Islamic law, which originates from the Koran.

In small towns, an ethnic leader or a respected priest, or *imam* (ee-MAAM), may be regarded as the governor of the town, but elected leaders similar to the mayors of the West are becoming more common.

The Libyan armed forces play an important role in politics. They have many officers who hold key positions on many of the popular committees.

During the 1980s, the zealous revolutionary committees terrorized the country. Thousands were arrested on suspicion. But gradually, Qadhafi was forced to admit that his system was not working. In 1988 the revolutionary committees were deprived of their power of arrest and imprisonment, which they had badly misused.

"Libya had no independent non-governmental organizations, human rights groups or independent bar association. Libyan law prohibits the formation of political parties and criticism of the political system. The press continues to be strictly controlled by the government."

—Amnesty International's annual report on Libya, 2002

As a result, the General People's Congress (GPC) was formed and given supreme power in the government. It had the power to sign treaties and declare war with other countries. The Congress elects the General People's Committee, the cabinet, and the revolutionary head or head of state.

The GPC also approved a charter of human rights, promising freedom of expression and condemning violence. Qadhafi's popularity with the masses increased as a result. The army and police force were abolished and replaced by a force of Jamahiriya Guards supervised by people's defense committees.

Jamahiriya Guards at a parade.

The prime minister's office in Tripoli, which is also part of the office of the People's Congress.

PEOPLE'S CONGRESS

Libya is strongly socialist. The government in Libya works through a national network of congresses and committees that are democratically elected by every citizen over the age of 18, whether male or female. In other words, ordinary people are encouraged and expected to play their part in government.

Over 2,000 of the local People's Congresses appoint higher-ranked Popular Committees that send resolutions to the GPC. These, in turn,

THE LIBYAN ARMED FORCES

In August 1989 it was announced that the traditional armed forces had been abolished. In future, they would be known as the armed people. That did not put an end to military service. Libyan men are still required to train three years in the army or four years in the navy or air force.

In 2002 Libya's armed forces were estimated to number 76,000. The 50,000-strong army, of which 40,000 were reservists in the People's Militia, was equipped with Russian-made tanks. The navy, with 8,000 personnel, had two Russian F-class submarines and various

frigates and coastal patrol crafts. The air force, employing 18,000 people, had more than 400 Russian- and French-made combat aircraft and 56 attack helicopters.

For all Qadhafi's well-publicized statements that military power was in the hands of the people, there are still many uniforms in the streets and plenty of military personnel on the most powerful committees. The original revolutionary council of army officers is no more, but most Libyans still consider the country a military state. An elaborate state security system penetrates all Libyan life. There have been at least nine coup attempts to remove Qadhafi from power. The regime's human rights record is full of reports of torture, disappearances, and executions of anyone believed to pose a threat to the dictator's regime.

pronounce the will of the people. National policy is directed by the GPC and administered by a series of secretariats. Each secretariat sends a secretary to the GPC, in much the same way as a cabinet in other democratic countries is made up of ministers from the different departments of government.

Though the political and economic capital of Libya is Tripoli, since 1988 all but two of the secretariats of the GPC have been relocated to other parts of the country.

ECONOMY

FOR CENTURIES, Libya was one of the poorest countries in the world. Farming produced just enough for people to live on, and the vast stretches of desert were not very useful to anyone except the nomads.

POVERTY TO WEALTH

In 1959 the discovery of oil changed Libya's fortunes. The increase in the price of oil in the 1970s made Libya the richest country in Africa. The oil industry provided employment and a high income for many Libyans.

However, the U.S. trade embargo with Libya, which began in 1982, and the UN sanctions in 1992 had a devastating effect on the economy. The standard of living declined rapidly and basic materials and food became scarce. Qadhafi's attempts to make Libya self-sufficient met little success and although a few countries continued to trade with Libya, there was widespread discontent. When the United Nations suspended sanctions in 1999, life for Libyans improved as the economy began to recover.

Libya's rapid population growth has reduced the overall wealth of the country. The population has climbed to 5.5 million, and if the current growth rate continues, the economy will not be able to provide enough jobs for young Libyans.

Opposite: **A crane block in an oil field located off Libya's western coast.**

Below: **Shepherds round up the sheep on a small farm south of Tobruk.**

43

The offshore oil platform of el-Bouri.

PETROLEUM

Libya's deserts conceal the largest underground reserves of oil in Africa and the eighth largest in the world. The reserves amount to about 30 billion barrels of oil. Libyan crude oil is particularly popular because it has little sulphur; it causes less pollution and is less expensive to process into petroleum.

In the 1960s, when these reserves were first tapped, Libya was the greatest oil producer in Africa. By 1965 Libya was the sixth largest exporter in the world, and in 1969 its oil output exceeded even Saudi Arabia's. Libya's oil production was severely restricted as a result of UN trade sanctions, but since the sanctions were suspended in 1999, many European and Arab countries have resumed drilling and refining operations in the country. The countries include Saudi Arabia, South Korea, Germany, Italy, Spain, and Canada.

Qadhafi has invested heavily in Libya's oil refineries and pipelines. Oil and petroleum products make up more than 97 percent of exports and account for a large number of jobs in industry and construction. Libya has three refineries capable of handling about 340,000 barrels a day. Pipelines up to 180 miles (290 km) long stretch from the oil fields, mostly in the desert off the Gulf of Sirte, to tanker terminals on the coast.

During the Iran-Iraq war in the 1980s, oil prices skyrocketed, only to collapse in 1986. Although by that time all Libyan oil had been nationalized so no foreign company could make a profit, the drop in price badly affected Libya's economy. Fresh reserves of offshore oil and natural gas were found near Banghazi in the 1990s. They have contributed further to Libya's oil wealth. It is possible present oil reserves in Libya could run out within 50 years. Qadhafi is reported to have said that "oil is a curse." He thinks the hope of quick riches has stifled any willingness for hard work among Libyans.

INDUSTRY

Libya boasts iron and steel complexes, an aluminum plant, and chemical complexes for natural salts. The most important industries in the public sector are processed foods (popular local products include canned tomato paste and tuna), soft drinks, tobacco, clothing, footwear, leather, wood, chemicals, and metal goods. Although in the past many factories were small and did not employ more than a hundred people, with heavy investment in large-scale complexes industry now supports 29 percent of the workforce. Esparto grass is a commercial crop, and a state-controlled factory processes it for export. There are also factories making rugs and cloth from imported materials.

The emphasis on petroleum and industry has resulted in an increase in the number of Libyans living near Tripoli and Banghazi. Both these cities are surrounded by slums as well as military installations. The population drift to the towns has caused serious problems. As in other countries, urban migration has led to housing shortages, and health and lifestyle have suffered. As there are not enough skilled laborers, Libya requires many foreign workers, who often claim the best salaries and houses.

AGRICULTURE

Until the discovery of oil, agriculture was Libya's main economic activity.

For centuries, the main economic activity in Libya was agriculture. However, things changed after the discovery of oil. The petroleum business produced get-rich-quick dreams among Libyans. There has been a growing flood of migrants from the farms to the towns. In 1960 about 70 percent of the population worked on the land; today the figure stands at less than 17 percent. Even the commercial farmers live in city houses and travel out each day to their farms on the Al-Jifarah Plain.

Farming produces only 7 percent of Libya's gross domestic product, and the yield per acre is the lowest of all North African countries. Nevertheless, improved irrigation has brought more areas under cultivation, and farmers are encouraged to use cooperative methods. The main crops are wheat, olives, barley, dates, peanuts, and citrus fruits. All are grown near the coast except dates and figs, which are grown in the oases. There are serious shortages of flour, rice, and non-citrus fruits.

SOUK TO SUPERMARKET

If you go shopping in Tripoli you will notice the absence of valuable articles such as handcrafted metalwork, quality leather goods, and Persian carpets. The gold jewelry for which Tripoli became famous is no more. Shoppers can look in vain for the Souk of the Perfumers or the Souk of the Saddlers and Leatherworkers. The principal imports are food products such as sugar, tea, and coffee, as well as construction materials and consumer goods.

In 1981 Qadhafi tried to close all privately-owned shops. He considered merchants "parasites" who produced nothing themselves but made money from the masses. So he encouraged the workers to seize control. They did. Most businesses with more than five employees are now controlled by a workers' committee. Qadhafi wanted people to shop only at state-registered supermarkets.

The system failed badly. Poor organization and interference by state committees caused bottlenecks in supply. Basic goods became unobtainable. Shopping was done on the black market. Gigantic state factories continued to create expensive goods nobody wanted to buy. In 1983 more than two-thirds of the country's food had to be imported; this included 800,000 tons of cereals. By 1985 Qadhafi was urging Libyans to eat camel meat to reduce the amount of beef and mutton being imported. It is hardly surprising that one of Libya's present aims is to be self-sufficient in food production.

Eventually, the lack of small businesses was recognized as a problem, and in 1988 the private sector (mostly partnerships offering employment to a community) was reestablished. Many businesses reopened and food products were easier to find, but it was not enough to ensure a steady supply of goods to the cities. More than two decades later, Libya still imports 75 percent of its food.

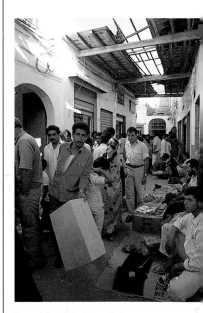

A souk is an Arab market filled with small, privately run stores or stalls that sell everything under the sun.

47

THE GREAT MAN-MADE RIVER

Since 1984 an enormous project has been underway to bring water to Libya's coastal regions from underground reserves in the south. This has been named the Great Man-Made River. Some 2,500 miles (4,000 km) of pipeline will carry water from ancient aquifers (sand layers that store water) in the Sahara Desert to irrigate 289 square miles (749 square km) of land and thus increase the local food supply. Corrosive salts in certain parts of the desert could attack the concrete pipeline, so coal-tar epoxy paints coat the outside of the pipes in these regions.

The pipes are 13 feet (4 m) in diameter, large enough to drive a car through. The project aims to pump 200 cubic feet (6 cubic m) of water a day to the major agricultural areas. The first stage, supplying the regions around Banghazi, was finished in 1991. The second stage, which provides Tripoli and its surrounding area with water from the desert aquifers, was inaugurated in 1997. Construction on the third stage continues, and completion of the entire project is expected in 2009.

Although the Great Man-Made River is impressive, experts think that the water table in the areas from which the water is being pumped may drop, threatening the supply to local oases. There is little hope of these deep water reserves being replenished if depleted. The thick, sandy dunes of the Sahara have so far protected underground water supplies from evaporation, but there is not sufficient rainfall to replenish them if they disappear. Within a century, they could run dry.

TRANSPORTATION

More than one-third of Libya's 15,180 miles (24,484 km) of road are paved. Most Libyans travel by bus. Cars are very expensive because they are all imported. U.S. makes are banned. Libya had a functioning railroad until 1965, when it was dismantled. In the 1990s the Libyan government began to build two railroad lines. One will travel from the Tunisian border to Tripoli and Mistratah, then stretch south to the desert town of Sabha, where iron ore is mined. The other will link the Egyptian border to the coastal town of Tobruk. Although planned for completion in 1994, both lines are not yet finished, although an Egyptian and a Spanish company have been hired to supply parts.

Traffic in downtown Banghazi.

Modern office blocks in Tripoli.

MODERN LIVING

For years, posters have proclaimed "a house for all" or "a car for all." This dream is fast approaching reality for many urbanites, although the house may be no more than an apartment in a hastily constructed building.

Many Libyans no longer approve of Qadhafi's dream. They think there is little point in working toward personal wealth when there is no stability in the country. The society created by Qadhafi's high ideals is riddled with incompetence, corruption, and apathy. Few officials on the hundreds of committees are willing to take responsibility for decisions, as many have been arrested for "failing" the new society. The ordinary citizen finds it difficult to obtain an official guarantee on anything.

In May 1980 a new currency was introduced. Anyone possessing more than US$2,100 worth of the old currency received no more than a receipt for the excess. All wealth has been collected by the state, to be redistributed when necessary. Many Libyans were found to have been hiding money in their houses.

Since UN sanctions were suspended in 1999, numerous foreign development projects have improved the quality of life in the country. Most Libyans have access to proper sewage, water, electricity and telephone services. Qadhafi places a high priority on his people's standard of living, and he is always making plans to improve facilities and services.

Water remains scarce, and a purification plant has been opened in Tobruk. Construction has begun on a huge desalination plant near Tripoli to purify seawater. However, in view of the escalating debts owed to foreign contractors, it seems unlikely that anything other than essential projects will be completed.

In 2000 the Italian government funded a center for agricultural experimentation in an effort to make Libya self-sufficient in food production. Still, the majority of foreign investment that has returned to Libya in recent years centers on improved access to oil and petroleum facilities.

"The agricultural revolution will enable the Libyan people to earn their living, to eat freely the food that was normally imported from overseas—this is freedom, this is independence, and this is the revolution."

—*Muammar Qadhafi, on the Great Man-Made River Project*

ONE MAN'S STORY

A Libyan named Saad worked hard and earned a scholarship to an agricultural college in Texas soon after World War II ended. In 1956 he returned to Libya, proud of the agricultural diploma he had received. He found that his new job as an agricultural adviser meant that he had to live in a remote village 40 miles (64 km) inland from Tripoli, where there was none of the high life he had tasted in the United States.

Then oil was discovered. The oil companies had an immediate need for educated Libyans. Saad found no difficulty in changing jobs for the better. Soon he was well off, married, and living in a six-room house.

The gap between city and country, and the educated and uneducated, remains wide. Libya has to pay high salaries to skilled immigrants with technical knowledge, as there are not enough qualified Libyans. Meanwhile, the poor remain desperately poor.

ENVIRONMENT

LIBYA IS MOSTLY DESERT, a difficulty for a nation that wants to produce enough food to feed its people. Qadhafi's dream of Libyan self-sufficiency is not only about agricultural production but includes industry and trade as well. Since Qadhafi came to power in 1969, the country has undergone intensive industrialization— when the government could pay for it. Projects such as the Great Man-Made River plan to transform the topography of the North African country but with serious consequences to the natural environment.

Some of the most arid areas of the Sahara Desert are found in Libya, where no animals or vegetation can survive. Droughts occur frequently and sometimes last as long as two years. It is no surprise that the country's main environmental issues revolve around water: its sources, its distribution, and its purity. Traditionally, Bedouin herders relied on regional wells and oases, but population pressures now place so much strain on the desert ecosystem that alternative sources of water must be found.

Libya's drive toward development does not always take into account the environmental consequences of rapid industrialization. Although the country has signed many international agreements, including those on desertification, climate change, marine dumping, and hazardous waste, progress does not always take into account the long-term effects of new projects. Many generations later, Libyans may find that what initially brought them prosperity has in fact made things worse.

Above: **Polluted skies over Tripoli and other big cities are one effect of industrialization.**

Opposite: **Scenery of the Fezzan desert in southwestern Libya.**

WATER

In a desert country brimming with oil wells and petroleum resources, water is a scarce commodity. On the coast, desalination plants remove dissolved minerals (mostly salt and other sediments) from Mediterranean seawater, but the process is expensive. One cubic meter of desalinated water costs several dollars to produce. In addition, desalination plants are extremely inefficient and extract only 15 to 50 percent fresh water from seawater.

In the 1960s a team searching for oil fields deep underground discovered a vast sea of aquifers under Libya's southern desert. Aquifers are great pools of fresh water trapped beneath layers of rock. Libya's southern aquifers were formed many thousands of years ago, when the Mediterranean Sea reached all the way to the Tibesti Mountains near Libya's border with Chad. Geological activity created the ranges of the Green Mountains, and basins were formed under the rocks beneath them. From 38,000 to 10,000 years ago, Libya had ample rainfall, and over the millennia, water gradually seeped through sedimentary rock to collect in the underground pools. The aquifers, undisturbed for ages, are now being drained to provide fresh water for Libya's cities and farms.

THE PRESSURES OF AGRICULTURE

With water so scarce, it is surprising that Libya can produce even a quarter of its food needs. In recent decades, many local aquifers have dried up and filled with salt water from the sea. Water tainted with salt and high in minerals kills crops and contaminates the entire aquifer.

Under the North African sun, evaporation rates are high. Half of all water used for irrigation is lost under the sun's burning rays. Traditional farming methods are inefficient, and much water is wasted during transportation or watering. To keep their land productive, Libyan farmers use 1,476 tons of fertilizer per square mile (570,000 kg per square km) of land—the 23rd highest use of fertilizer in the world. In 2003 Libya signed an agreement with the UN Food and Agricultural Organization (FAO) for more than $21 million of agricultural aid, which will modernize and improve seed production in the country.

Food accounts for 20 percent of Libya's imports. This creates dependence on the outside world. Qadhafi dreams of Libya being not only self-sufficient but also prosperous enough to export food, industrial goods, and development knowledge to Africa and the Middle East. Qadhafi wants Libya to return to being the bread basket of North Africa, a position it held in antiquity. That might not be realistic as climatic changes over the last 4,000 years have resulted in a steady increase in deserts.

Only little vegetation, such as pockets of drought-resistant plants, grows in the barren areas of Libya.

DESERT SPECIES

Most people mistakenly think the desert consists only of sand and rocks. The Sahara Desert, of which Libya is a part, has varied ecosystems of plant, animal, and insect life. Small plants germinate quickly after the rains, and fields of colorful flowers carpet the desert for days or weeks afterward. The plants must grow and reproduce quickly under the desert sun to escape dehydration and death. Still, seeds can lie buried under the Saharan sands for up to a decade until there is enough rain for growth, when once again the desert blooms.

Although the Libyan Desert is one of the hottest and driest areas of the Sahara, reptiles and insects have adapted well to the challenges of survival. Lizards and desert snakes burrow under the ground during the day to escape the hot desert sun but come out to bask in the gentle warmth of morning and evening. Scorpions burrow deep into the sand and impart a dangerous and sometimes lethal sting to anyone who unwittingly steps in their path. Around the desert oases there are mosquitoes, which breed in any stagnant water they can find and plague the population, even in one of the driest and most remote areas of the world.

Because of increased development and population pressure, the mammals of Libya face increased danger and many species are in decline. The famous Barbary lion of North Africa, used in bloody games at the Colosseum during the days of the Roman Empire, is now found only in special breeding areas. In the early 20th century it was hunted almost to extinction. Now there are none left in the wild. City people increasingly hunt the ibex, a small gazelle perfectly adapted to rocky and dry terrain, and they are quickly becoming an endangered species. Unfortunately, Libyans are not aware of the pressures they are placing on their environment or the plight of endangered animals that live within their borders. Many international organizations, such as the African Conservation Foundation and the World Wildlife Fund, are starting programs to save desert species.

THE GROWING DESERT

Ten thousand years ago, the deserts of Libya were green and lush with rolling plains and abundant wildlife. What is now the Sahara Desert even sported tropical rainforest high in the mountains. Scientists believe that 8,000 years ago, the Earth rotated slightly on its axis, with devastating results. The plains that had been fertile dried up and the desert rapidly claimed what had once been productive farmland. To this day, the process continues and desertification is a serious problem in Libya. Already, 95 percent of the country is desert and agricultural land is of poor quality.

Deserts and their borders are very fragile ecosystems. Any change in rainfall has a dramatic effect on vegetation. Desertification occurs when the area that borders a desert, called a transition zone, comes under pressure from increasing human population. Herds of livestock trample the plant life and harden the soil so it is more vulnerable to wind and rain erosion. Overgrazing destroys what is left. Firewood collection eventually destroys the trees. The deserts of Libya thus look destined for expansion.

In some areas of the Sahara, no rain falls for up to 200 consecutive days in a year.

57

THE FRAGILE SEA

Since the days of the early Phoenician settlers, life in Libya has revolved around the Mediterranean coast. Most oceans and seas filter waste and debris efficiently, although manmade pollutants such as plastics and metals are becoming an increasing problem.

The Mediterranean Sea is one of the most polluted bodies of water in the world. It is unable to renew itself because of its enclosed shape, which restricts water circulation and flushing. The sewage, plastic waste, oil runoffs, and chemical pollutants that are dumped in its waters daily cause increasing damage to the sea's fragile ecosystem. Libya has signed international agreements concerning marine dumping and wetlands preservation in an effort to protect its 1,100-mile (1,770-km) coastline from environmental pollution and contamination.

Right: **Various measures are now in place to protect the Mediterranean Sea from further pollution.**

Opposite: **A shipwreck near the coastal city of Talmitha.**

Of all the pollutants that threaten the Mediterranean Sea, oil causes the most permanent damage. Since 1983 it has been illegal to dump oil in the Mediterranean, but tankers traveling between the Black Sea, southern Europe, North Africa, and the Middle East continue to release excess oil residues. Experts estimate that up to 330,000 tons of oil are illegally dumped in the Mediterranean each year. Petroleum has many carcinogenic substances, and oil dumping causes immense damage to the tourism and fishing industries.

For centuries, the people of the Mediterranean coast have depended on the sea for survival. Libyan fishermen catch about 32,450 tons of fish in the Mediterranean Sea each year, but fish populations are declining due to the high oil residue of coastal waters. Modern fishing methods such as netting have resulted in overfishing in most areas and the marine populations are not given a chance to replenish their previously staggering numbers. Issues such as the dumping of open sewage and the harvesting of red coral for tourist curios contribute to the decline of marine life in the Mediterranean. In recent years, awareness of the sea's pollution has grown and the international community is taking action to protect its fragile waterways.

LIBYANS

ALMOST ALL LIBYANS TODAY are Arabic-speaking Muslims, descended from the Arabs who settled in the area during the last 1,200 years. Many of the early Arabs married into Berber families or into the families of the descendants of Roman or Greek colonists, so few Libyans today are of pure Arab descent. Some Libyans look like Turks or Egyptians, while others have the darker skin of the desert nomads.

Although the desert-separated areas of Tripolitania, Cyrenaica, and Fezzan have been one country since 1951, Libyans still tend to think tribally rather than nationally. The tribe is the basic unit of Libya's social structure and the *bayt* (bait)—the family within the tribe—is the social group to which they feel they belong.

Left: **A gathering of races in the Sirte Desert.**

Opposite: **A group of women walking in the old walled city, or medina, in Tripoli.**

MINORITY GROUPS

In the southern oases there are a few communities of pure Berber ancestry. Proud of their origins, they tend to live apart from other Libyans. There are some Libyans who think of themselves as Turkish, or descendants of Turkish soldiers who settled in the area in the days of the Ottoman empire.

Another minority group are the Sharifs, who live only in Fezzan oases and claim descent from Prophet Muhammad. There are black Africans from Sudan and countries south of the Sahara, many of them originally brought to Libya as slaves. Most are now Muslims and considered Libyans.

A few Maltese sponge fishers live on the coast. There were once small colonies of Italian farmers, who settled in Libya during the Italian occupation, but most of them have left due to Libyan resentment against their former occupiers.

Old Libyan Arabs.

AFRICAN ARABS

Some say that Arabs form as much as 97 percent of Libya's population, or over 5.3 million people, and that two-thirds of all Arabs in the world live in Africa. Yet most Libyans do not think of themselves as Arab, although they are proud of their strict adherence to Islam.

Most of Libya's population is crowded in the north near the Mediterranean coast where there is a greater chance for employment. More than 95 percent of Libyans live in Tripolitania and Cyrenaica, where they have a

Libyan Arabs in a town square.

better quality of life and good access to government services. Fewer than 5 percent of Libyans live in Fezzan, mostly Bedouin and other groups that can survive in the harsh desert region. On the Mediterranean coastal strip, Libyans are exposed to a modern lifestyle, Western ideas, and contact with foreign workers, but they are still strongly influenced by traditional Islamic customs.

Many Libyan families have been farmers for generations, although few produce more than just enough for their own small community to live on.

In the cities of Tripoli and Banghazi, one can see the sharp contrast between rich and poor, despite Qadhafi's claims of equal distribution of wealth. Senior army officers, administrators, directors of state companies, lawyers, and foreign technical experts all live in newly built suburbs where shops sell black-market goods from abroad.

The bulk of the people live in state-built apartment buildings that are short on space, light, and hygiene. They line up for food at the state-controlled supermarkets. On the outskirts of the cities are the spreading shanty towns.

THE BEDOUIN

Deep in the Libyan desert, there is a seminomadic group of people called the Bedouin. Their name means desert dwellers in Arabic. Their territory stretches from the vast deserts of North Africa to the rocky sands of the Middle East. Although they are divided into separate groups with their own territory, the Bedouin share a common culture of herding camels and goats. They measure their wealth by the number of animals in their herd and the quality of their thoroughbred Arabian horses. Bedouins live in family groups called clans and have to move their camps several times a year to find fresh grazing for their herds.

For centuries, the Bedouin have been known for their hospitality and courage. During medieval times, they often raided caravans and desert outposts for gold and other booty. During the Islamic empire, rulers found the Bedouin impossible to control and often let them rule themselves. Even today, the Bedouin enjoy a semi-autonomous existence in Libya.

Despite the Libyan government's attempts to organize the Bedouin, most prefer their traditional way of life in the desert. Even young Bedouin men who work in the cities return frequently to their camps in times of trial and celebration, and their roots remain strong.

Tuareg shepherds in the Sahara.

THE AMAZIGH

When the Arab invaders swept across North Africa in the seventh century, the fiercest resistance came from the northwest (now Tunisia, Algeria, and Morocco). The Arabs called the area Jazirat Al Maghreb, or the island of the west. The inhabitants of the area were Berbers, and their descendants still live in Libya. They are believed to be the original inhabitants of North Africa.

It is thought that the Berbers, also known as the Amazigh, once inhabited the entire northern half of the African continent. After the Arab invasion many Berbers converted to Islam. From the 11th to the 13th centuries, two Berber groups called the Almoravids and Almohads became powerful enough to build Islamic empires in northwestern Africa and Spain.

Berber children.

Now making up little more than 3 percent of the Libyan population, pure-blooded Berbers live in inaccessible mountain areas such as Jabal Nafusah and a few isolated oases in Fezzan where their ancestors retreated to escape the Arabs. They grow crops and keep herds of sheep and goats, often living a seminomadic life to find sufficient pasture.

Berbers consider themselves members of individual groups rather than a single nation. Most are Muslim and belong to the Kharijite sect of Islam. They revere local saints and holy places from their religious tradition.

The old Berber language and their reluctance to marry out of their group set them apart from other ethnic groups.

Berber women enjoy more personal freedom than Arab women. They had the right to own property, get a divorce, and remarry long before Muslim women gained such rights.

A member of the Tuareg.

PEOPLE OF THE BLUE VEIL

The Tuareg are a fiercely independent desert people who do not consider themselves as belonging to any particular country. The remaining Tuareg groups are found in Libya, northwestern Niger, and Mali. Many are still nomadic, but their ancient way of life is now restricted by national borders, so most have settled around oases.

The Tuareg can be distinguished from the white-clothed Berbers by their black or dark blue cloaks and are known as the People of the Blue Veil. The origin of the custom of wearing a veil grew from the need for protection from sand and sun, but it is also a mark of pride. In contrast to Islamic tradition, it is the Tuareg man who veils his face; the woman is not so bound, though she will usually cover her mouth in the presence of strangers or her father-in-law. Property is inherited by children through the mother, not the father.

Like the Bedouin, the Tuareg were notorious for raiding settlements and stealing cattle. The Tuareg once achieved brief Hollywood fame as the "bad guys" in the movie *Beau Geste*. They speak their own language, which they write in their own ancient alphabet. Part of Tuareg society are the black African *iklan* (ik-LAWN) who were originally slaves captured during raids across the Niger.

THE MODERN LIBYAN

The change in Libya from a largely nomadic society to a modern consumer society has been rapid. The inflation rate in 2003 was about 2.5 percent. People are discontented, streets are dirty, and food is scarce. At times, markets run out of fruit and vegetables. Meat, eggs, and butter are equally hard to find. Libyans display a grim defiance toward threats from abroad but take no delight in their lifestyle.

Since 1980 any outspoken opposition to Qadhafi's theories of the ideal socialist Arab state has been ruthlessly punished. Many people in the business community have reportedly been arrested or had their property confiscated under anti-corruption laws introduced in 1994. The job of confiscating assets was carried out by Purification Committees, which were made up of young military officers and students. It is also believed that hundreds of people have been sent to prison for political reasons. Today's Libyans are adapting their desire for privacy into a withdrawal from anything that could be construed as political comment.

Forced by Qadhafi's "democracy" to partake in endless committees, Libyans procrastinate rather than make decisions that could cause them problems later. They retreat increasingly into the reassurance of their religion. The Jamahiriya's ideal society, which seemed so successful in the days of oil wealth, has become a state-dominated oppression.

Modern Libyan women.

An immigrant who works at the Commonwealth War Cemetery in Tobruk.

IMMIGRANT WORKERS

Libya's history of colonization and invasions has made Libyans suspicious of foreigners. Foreigners have at various times been banned from working in Libya. During the UN sanctions, Qadhafi ordered nearly all Americans and Europeans to leave the country, but after 1999 European companies were once again encouraged to invest in Libya. For the most part, Americans remain unwelcome because the U.S. government continues to impose a trade embargo on Libya. The suspension of sanctions by the United Nations in 1999 produced an increase in the number of foreigners working in Libya. They are valued for their expertise in technical fields, as few Libyans have such expertise. The foreigners include Italians, Germans, Britons, Thais, Koreans, and Indians.

Libya recruits technical workers from abroad to produce oil, construct irrigation networks, and advise on sophisticated military equipment. Foreigners with such skills earn good wages. More than 2 million foreigners are estimated to be working in the country.

WHAT TO WEAR?

For centuries, style and clothing throughout the Middle East and across Africa were dictated by Islamic tradition. Men wore long white robes that kept them cool during the day. They also wore a rope-bound head scarf or wound turban. The way the turban was knotted was a clear indication of the area in which one lived. Women also wore robes to preserve their modesty, an important virtue in Islamic society. From the age of puberty, they kept their faces veiled whenever men were present, and married women often wore black to denote their marital status.

Gradually, the styles of the West arrived. The red Turkish fez and European suits spread through the Mediterranean Arab world and to Libya. Apart from the Arabic posters, shop names, and road signs, there is little difference between the streets of Tripoli or Banghazi and those in almost any Mediterranean port. Girls wear bright-colored dresses, often with dark-colored trousers beneath for modesty; boys wear shirts and jeans.

College students and young married couples tend to wear modern clothes: an open-necked shirt in summer, a turtleneck in winter, with a leather jacket or zipped parka for men. Women still wear a head scarf, even with a blouse and skirt.

Traditional dresses are long and flowing, and worn with charms and necklaces that are believed to protect the wearer from evil spells. Koranic verses are also worn around the neck. Army uniforms are visible, as are modern suits with shirt and tie and traditional Arab robes for older people. Young men go bareheaded; others wear a black or white Islamic cap.

South of the coastal cities, people wear the Arab robes of Islamic tradition. The robes are white, loose and flowing, and are more comfortable to wear in the hot desert climate as they trap the wind and reflect the sunlight.

A man in typical Libyan attire.

LIFESTYLE

WEALTH from the oil industry brought social challenges as the income gap between the rich and poor widened dramatically. However, one thing that did not change was religion. Islam remains central to Libya's way of life. Indeed, recent years have seen Qadhafi enforcing an even stricter interpretation of the Islamic code.

Islamic life is bound by tradition. Families in Libya dress mainly in traditional clothes. They attend the mosque regularly, and each day is structured around the five prayer times. People stay close to home in the evening. Pocket money is not wasted on soft drinks or cigarettes. No one goes out for a drink. Alcohol is forbidden and there are no bars or nightclubs. Even the innumerable cafés, selling cups of sweet, strong coffee and local fizzy drinks, are threatened by a shortage of basic food products.

Friday is the Islamic holy day, as Saturday is for Jews and Sunday for Christians. Muslims go to the mosque at noon on Fridays to join in public prayer and on other days if time permits.

However, the Libyan way of life in urban areas along the coast is modern and liberal when compared to the centuries-old lifestyle inland. Working in the fields or tending the animals is considered a reward in itself. People in those areas have been forced to live that way not because of religion but because of the environment.

Opposite: **Shoppers at a souk in Tripoli.**

Below: **Workers about to close a shoe shop for the day and go for evening prayers.**

71

HOMES

The traditional home of a prosperous Libyan family is built to an accepted pattern. Behind a stout wooden door is a corridor leading to a bright patio. The rooms of the house are grouped around this open-air square, which often has a pool or fountain in the middle. The square is the focal point for family activities. The rooms have plain, whitewashed walls, but the floors are decorated with carpets and tasseled cushions on low benches. Some houses also have intricately-designed tiles and ceilings.

Almost-completed high-rise blocks in Tripoli.

The days of such lavish styles, which go back to the days of the Umayyad empire in the eighth century, are passing. Most city-dwellers live in apartment buildings. Color-washed walls are cheaper than Persian carpets, though families like to have rugs if they can afford them. A low couch along one wall is common, and embroidered cushions take the place of armchairs. There will be a picture of Qadhafi. The kitchen area is traditionally the woman's private domain.

Farther inland, many houses are built of mud bricks. Mud walls are perfectly suited to the desert climate because they keep the house cool during summer and trap warm air during the coldest months of winter.

Most houses have only one floor, with a flat roof and sometimes moulded pinnacles on each corner. They have very small windows—partly for privacy and partly because the walls are stronger that way. Fancier homes in the cities are built around a central courtyard. Narrow alleyways between the houses provide shade.

A WOMAN'S LIFE

Islamic society is patriarchal—familes are headed by the father figure. For years in Libya, only boys went to school. No one could see any point in educating girls, who were expected to become wives and mothers.

In Libya, women have had the right to vote and run for public office since 1963, but few choose to do so. Qadhafi has tried to change the inferior status of women by passing legislation that gives them equal rights. They have access to education and employment, but most choose jobs dominated by women such as nursing, teaching, social work, and secretarial work. Islamic law in Libya denies women custody of children, alimony payments, and equal inheritance after divorce.

A Libyan woman prepares to sing.

It is very important in Libyan society for women to be modest. Only a woman's hands, feet, and face can be left uncovered in public, and to disregard these conventions is a serious offence against family honor. Within an Arab group, a man's reputation depends largely on the behavior of the women in his family. Most girls start wearing the traditional black cloak and veil at puberty, but in some families even 6-year-old girls cover their heads.

Many Libyan women work outside the home. Raising children and taking care of the house remain as women's responsibilities, however, and most women in Libya stay home at least when their children are very young. More traditional families restrict a woman's outdoor movements to only the most essential activities. Nevertheless, times are changing in Libya, and as the country liberalizes, the strict Islamic values that have governed life there for centuries are slowly relaxing.

CHILDREN

Children are extremely valued in the Arab world. Most people cannot imagine life without marriage and many children. Traditionally, the birth of a woman's first child raised her status to that of a full-fledged member of the community, but that is changing as more women seek employment and fulfillment outside the home.

Most Muslim babies have their heads shaved because of religious customs, and male babies are circumcised. However, sometimes the family decides to wait and incorporates the circumcision into an important ceremony when the boy is 10 or 11.

An enthusiastic group of children.

Libyan children grow up accepting that all important decisions will be made by their father. Children in the Arab world, especially in rural areas, have much more responsibility than children in the West. Although they have ample time to play and joke with their young relatives and friends, they help with household chores and often take care of their younger siblings. They are treated as small adults, expected to help the family once they are no longer toddlers. In Fezzan families, young girls care for the babies while their mother is out, milk the goats, and fetch water from the well.

EDUCATION

School is compulsory in Libya for children aged 6 to 15. Lessons are taught exclusively in Arabic. Besides Arabic, schoolchildren study the Koran and Islamic teaching and traditions. The syllabus for older children includes other subjects such as history, geography, and science.

Libyan boys attend special religious classes after school. They listen to the Koran being recited and memorize the verses. A few private schools cater to children from wealthy families.

Libyans can further their education at the established universities of Garyounis in Banghazi and Al Fatah in Tripoli or at the new universities in Sabha and Marsa al Burayqah. There are also agricultural, technical, and vocational training institutes.

In 1951, at the time of independence, nearly 90 percent of the Libyan population was illiterate, and there were no girls in the intermediate and high schools. In 2003 more than 80 percent of the population was literate, and 72 percent of women could read and write.

The Al Fatah college in Tripoli.

MARRIAGE

According to Islamic law, a man can have up to four wives at one time, but he must provide each with equal possessions and give each an equal amount of his time. Today, most Libyans marry only once.

In spite of the modern trend toward marrying for love, most Libyan marriages are still arranged by the couple's parents. But the couple often know each other before the wedding. Family connections, social class, education, and employment status all count in choosing a spouse.

The marriage ceremony in the Arab world does not take place in a mosque. Instead, the mosque's cleric, or *imam*, goes to the groom's house to write out the marriage contract. Once the document is signed, family and friends rejoice, dance, and sing. The bride is led to her husband's house in a joyous procession. Celebrations continue with a huge banquet.

In Islam, marriage is a religious duty and children are considered a blessing from God. For the Bedouin, marriage was a means of strengthening connections and forming alliances between families.

In traditional Islamic law, a husband is allowed to divorce his wife by saying "I divorce you" three times in front of two witnesses. Since 1973 women have had equal rights in obtaining a divorce, but they have been reluctant to use it because of the social stigma it brings. Nevertheless, divorce is now more socially accepted in the Arab world, and it is common for both the man and woman to remarry.

A bride on her special day.

76

BEDOUIN HOSPITALITY AND HONOR

The ancient traditions of Bedouin hospitality arise from the harsh conditions of the desert. The Bedouin believe thats if a stranger comes to their tent dying of thirst, they should give the stranger food and shelter for three days, even if the stranger might have murdered a member of their family.

Bedouin hosts brew fresh coffee for their guests and the family drinks whatever is left later. They use beautiful brass jugs that may be among the family's most prized possessions to serve their guests. In the cities, people offer their guests a cup of tea or coffee. Owners of traditional shops do the same for their customers, but the practice does not fit the fast-paced supermarket culture of the cities.

While the Bedouin regard hospitality as a duty and offer it freely to any visitor, they guard their honor fiercely and jealously. Upholding honor may mean death, as an insult can start a blood feud. Robbery and theft are not common in Bedouin society. People respect one another's property, and a Bedouin family can safely leave their rolled-up tent weighted with stones on the ground without worry of it being stolen while they are away.

HEALTH

Qadhafi's socialist government has instituted free health services and increased facilities dramatically. Before the UN sanctions, Libya had one of the best healthcare systems in Africa. But when medicines and supplies became difficult to obtain, the quality rapidly declined. Today, educated professionals who have the opportunity to leave Libya emigrate to work elsewhere.

There are two big hospitals, in Tripoli and Banghazi, and many smaller hospitals and clinics around the country, while mobile health units visit the country districts.

Some schools provide health services and supplement the children's diet, and there are some mother-and-child care centers. Instead of the Red Cross, there are clinics run by the Red Crescent Society as it is called in Islamic countries.

In the years following the revolution from 1969 to 1978, the number of doctors in Libya increased by between four and five times. The increase slowed down dramatically after UN sanctions were imposed. After 1999 access to medicine, machinery, and materials increased and healthcare facilities expanded. Today, there are more than 20,000 hospital beds and about 7,000 physicians in Libya.

There are few training facilities for doctors and nurses within Libya, so most doctors are foreigners or foreign-trained. Traditions that prevent married women from coming into contact with any man other than their husband have made it hard for Libyan women to be trained as nurses or doctors, but the situation is beginning to change.

The main health problems in Libya are tuberculosis, intestinal diseases caused by unhygienic drinking water, and eye diseases (such as trachoma). Age-old scourges such as typhoid and leprosy are still present, but malaria has been wiped out with the aid of the World Health Organization.

DEATH AND BURIAL

Libyan children are brought up not to be frightened by the idea of death. Muslims believe that everything comes from God and, however difficult circumstances may be, everything happens for the best. It is considered holy to face life's trials calmly and without complaint. Certainly the Bedouin meet death all too often in the harsh desert.

No Libyan family would ever put an aged relative into an old-age home. They are glad to have them at home, where they can turn to them for advice. With their family around them, the elderly accept the approach of death in a dignified manner. A Libyan might well gather friends and relatives and say farewell to each one before he or she dies.

A cemetery in Tripoli.

According to tradition, the dead body is washed in water or sand. It is then clothed in fresh linen and buried in a shallow grave. The custom is to lay the corpse facing Mecca. In the desert, few people attend this ceremony. In the towns, many do, anxious to help carry the body. Women are not allowed to be part of the funeral procession as it is believed that they are too emotional. Exaggerated expressions of grief are not allowed in Islam. For ordinary people, no monuments or headstones are used. Muslims believe that once a person is dead, the body is of no further use.

RELIGION

TO UNDERSTAND THE PEOPLE OF LIBYA, one must understand their religion, because religion governs their lives, their education, their language, and their hopes for the future.

LIBYA AND SUNNI ISLAM

The religion of Libya is Islam, which means submission to the will of Allah. Allah is the word Muslims use for God, who is considered compassionate and merciful but who cannot be fully known. Islam is divided into two sects: about 90 percent of the total Muslim population are members of the Sunni sect; the rest belong to the Shi'a sect. Most Libyans are Sunni (SOO-nee) Muslims.

Islam is a practical religion with clear rules for living and worship. Africa has historical and political ties to the Middle East, where Islam continues to be a popular religion. About 20 percent of the world's 1 billion Muslims are found in Africa.

Since the 1969 revolution, everything Arabic and Islamic in Libya has been intensified, while anything considered contrary to Islamic beliefs is destroyed or forbidden. Qadhafi has strongly encouraged conversions to Islam in African countries such as Nigeria.

Opposite: **One of the newer mosques in Ghadamis.**

Below: **Libyan children inside a mosque.**

PROPHET MUHAMMAD

Muhammad, the founder of Islam, was born in Mecca, a prosperous trading town in today's Saudi Arabia, in A.D. 570, more than five centuries after the birth of Jesus Christ. After Muhammad's father died, his mother could not afford to look after him, so he was sent to live with his grandfather in the desert. He started as a herdboy and later worked for his uncle, traveling with the camel caravans.

At the age of 25 he married a woman called Khadija, who became one of his staunchest supporters. They had six children, but Muhammad's surviving descendants were all children of his daughter, Fatimah.

As Muhammad traveled, he became aware of Judaism and Christianity. He also knew how many people in Arabia still worshiped idols. He traveled into the mountains, where he began having dreams and visions. Muslims believe that while in the mountains, Muhammad heard the words of God spoken to him by the angel Gabriel. Although Muhammad himself could not read or write, he told others what he had heard. The words were written down and became the holy book of Islam, the Koran.

When Muhammad took his words to Mecca in the hope that people there would turn to Allah, he met with fierce opposition. In 622, preceded by about 70 men and their families, he migrated to a town farther north called Medina, where the people welcomed his arrival. There, he built the first mosque.

By 629, after years of fierce fighting between the two towns, Muhammad's support was strong enough for him to lead his forces into Mecca. The square enclosure that had once housed idols became the sacred Ka'bah (kah-AH-bah), the central shrine of pilgrimage for Muslims.

Muhammad died in 632 and was buried at Medina. Muslims do not worship Muhammad, but he is respected and honored as God's last prophet.

THE FIVE PILLARS OF ISLAM

Every true Muslim accepts five basic religious duties:

1. *Shahada* (sha-HAD-ah)—the confession of faith. To bear witness that there is no god other than Allah and that Muhammad is his final messenger and prophet.

2. *Salat* (sahl-AHT)—prayer. To pray five times daily, facing the direction of Mecca, at daybreak, noon, mid-afternoon, after sunset, and early in the night.

3. *Zakat* (za-KAHT)—alms giving. To give 2.5 percent of one's annual earnings to the poor and needy.

4. Fasting in the month of Ramadan (rah-mah-DAHN). To go without food or drink between dawn and sunset for the 30 days of the lunar month.

5. Hajj—pilgrimage. To make the pilgrimage to Mecca once in a lifetime.

Muslims also have six main beliefs as the foundation of their faith. They believe that Allah is the only god and there exist angels, holy books, prophets, the Day of Judgment, and predestiny.

Apart from the five daily prayers, impromptu prayers are also offered with open palms at feasts, on special occasions, or in remembrance of loved ones. Women may also offer prayers in a special section of the mosque or in the privacy of their homes.

An elderly Sunni Muslim.

SHI'ISM

Shi'ites are the second largest Islamic sect in Libya. Shi'a Muslims broke away from the dominant Sunnis for reasons of theology and politics. One difference stems from arguments over Muhammad's successors as caliphs, the spiritual leaders of Muslims. The Shi'ites wanted the caliphate to descend through Ali, Muhammad's son-in-law. Ali eventually became the fourth caliph, but he was murdered soon after. Since then, the Shi'ites have accused the later caliphs, whom the Sunnis followed, of being usurpers.

Shi'ites also regard their holy men as having far greater authority than ordinary Muslims. This opposes the Sunni belief that their religious leaders are ordinary Muslims who have received extra training as teachers and leaders in prayer.

PLACE OF PRAYER

A mosque is a place of worship, as a church is. Indeed, many buildings have been used as one and then the other. Structurally, the greatest difference is that a Christian worshiper usually enters a church at one end of the building to see the altar at the far end, whereas a Muslim more often enters the mosque in the middle of one of the long walls and faces across.

While churches were traditionally built with the altar at the eastern end (for most of Europe, the eastern end pointed to Jerusalem, where Jesus was crucified and resurrected), mosques are oriented so that worshipers directly face Mecca, the sacred city of Islam.

Every mosque needs a tower from which the muezzin or mosque official can give the call to prayer. Often the towers are in the shape of a slender minaret, with hundreds of steps leading to the top. Today, a muezzin usually uses a loudspeaker system, made essential by the clamor of the modern city. The muezzin were once chosen from among the blind, so that they could concentrate on the prayer and not be distracted by the view from the top of the minaret.

A running fountain in the courtyard is also an essential facility for worshipers, because Islam prescribes that people cleanse themselves with water before they pray. Some mosques even have a bath house, similar to a Turkish bath, attached.

WITHIN THE BUILDING

To people who are used to ornate, furnished Christian churches, a mosque may seem empty. Whether large or small, the mosque is essentially an open space covered with carpets for the kneeling worshipers.

There are only two particular features. In the eastern wall is an empty recess called the *mihrab* (mi-RAHB), which indicates the direction of Mecca. There is also the *minbar* (MIN-bar), or pulpit, often in the shape of a narrow flight of steps, from which the *imam* leads prayers and preaches.

No images or pictures adorn the walls or pillars because Islam forbids the depiction of living creatures, but they are often resplendent with artistic shapes, colorful tiles, geometric designs, and Arabic calligraphy.

The decorated walls, the rich carpets, the stained-glass windows, and the architectural symmetry all combine to contribute to an atmosphere of holy splendor.

Inside the Gurgi Mosque in Tripoli.

The Sidi Addi Wahab Mosque in Tripoli.

PILGRIMAGE TO MECCA

Once a small desert town visited only by caravans of camels, Mecca is now a major city in Saudi Arabia and the holiest place of Islam. It had some importance even before the birth of Muhammad. A black stone, probably a meteorite, was said to have been sent by God. The black stone was built into the wall of a square enclosure that housed a profusion of idols. That square building is the Ka'bah. Today it is draped with a ceremonial black cloth embroidered with gold called the *kiswah* (KEYS-wa). The Great Mosque has been built around the Ka'bah.

Mecca is now an endlessly crowded town among sheltering hills. Muslim pilgrims on their annual pilgrimage are expected to camp in the desert as Muhammad once did, but that has not prevented Mecca from becoming a town of hotels and souvenir shops. Traffic is an increasing problem and there are plans to build elevated bypass roads. Visitors arrive by air or through the adjoining port of Jiddah on the Red Sea.

SUPERSTITIONS

Islamic tradition frowns on superstition. Nevertheless, Muslims pay great attention to dreams, which they believe are sent by God. In many communities there are people known for their ability to interpret dreams. Most Libyans believe that dreams have an opposite result. For example, a frightening dream may well be a good sign. Dreams can also be warnings of dire happenings, although such events cannot be avoided—they are "the will of Allah."

Muslims believe that sickness may be sent by God, or through the power of a curse from someone wishing another harm. Many Libyans wear charms, usually a small container with a verse from the Koran, on a leather thong. Some pregnant women wear an earring in the shape of a blue hand with an eye on its palm. The hand is called the *khamsa* (KHAHM-sa), or the hand of Fatima, and is meant to protect the wearer from harm and bad luck.

Some older Libyans believe in the existence of evil spirits called jinn that live in haunted places. They can drive a person insane or kill them. Jinn are believed to be able to assume the form of snakes, dogs, cats, monsters, or people.

"He who helps a Muslim in his worldly distress will be rewarded by Allah on the day of judgment."

—*Prophet Muhammad*

GENIES AND SPELLS

Strict Muslims like to hear stories from the Koran and on the life of Prophet Muhammad. Many Libyans also enjoy listening to folktales passed down for many generations that tell of enchanted lands and the spirit world. Many of the fables have a hero who encounters a genie or another type of magical creature that helps him win his fortune. The hero also often meets mythical creatures such as winged birds and fierce monsters, and wicked sorcerers who cast evil spells. Although such stories are frowned upon by strict Islamic tradition, they are very popular with Libyans.

THE HAJJ

Every year, about 2 million Muslims, including many Libyans, make the pilgrimage to Mecca in Saudi Arabia. To make this journey is an honor, a blessing, and the greatest longing of any Muslim.

Enormous camps surround Mecca at the time of the pilgrimage. Everyone wears similar clothing, so there is no distinction between rich and poor. Men wear two pieces of seamless white cloth, one wrapped around the lower body, the other draped over the shoulder. Women wear green underclothes and a cloak and veil.

The first task, immediately after arrival in Mecca, is to walk around the walls of the Great Mosque. Then the pilgrims join the throng inside the mosque to walk seven times around the Ka'bah. If possible, they kiss the black stone built into its outside wall, said to be a stone on which Abraham once stood. Next comes the visit to drink from the sacred well of Zamzam, where prayers and ceremonials are recited.

On the eighth day, the pilgrims move to the Mount of Mercy, about 13 miles (21 km) from Mecca. There, Muhammad once gave a famous sermon. The pilgrims stand or sit in meditation from midday to sunset. The shelter of an umbrella is permitted if the hajj falls during the intense heat of summer. This visit is considered so important that if it is omitted the pilgrimage is considered to have no value.

At sunset, they move to Mina, where three stone pillars representing the devil stand. In Muhammad's time, the three pillars belonged to a popular temple for goddess worship that was demolished when he returned with his followers to Mecca.

On the 10th day, the end of the hajj is marked by the great Feast of Sacrifice. It is a time for giving alms, for prayers and rejoicing, for sermons in the open air, and for the sacrifice of a lamb, goat, cow, or camel. The

"Say to the believing men that they should lower their gaze and guard their modesty; that will make for greater purity for them; and Allah is well acquainted with all that they do. And say to the believing women that they should lower their gaze and guard their modesty; that they should not display their beauty and ornaments except what (must ordinarily) appear thereof; that they should draw their veils over their bosoms and not display their beauty."

—the Koran

feast officially lasts three days, but the celebrations often continue for a full week.

Each pilgrim washes, cuts off ceremonial locks of hair, and puts on new clothes to symbolize the entering of a new life. After that some pilgrims go back to the Ka'bah for a farewell circling. Before leaving Saudi Arabia, the pilgrim may visit Medina, where Muhammad built his first mosque and where he is buried.

The return of the pilgrims is another cause for celebrations. Many Libyans paint their houses with murals of the pilgrimage, and their neighbors come to congratulate them.

FOOD AND FASTING

An essential principle of Islam is submission to God, and a Muslim's diet must also conform to the will of God. In Libya, the Islamic diet is strictly observed.

Alcohol is forbidden in any form. It may not be brought into Libya by visitors, whether or not they are Muslim. As in Judaism, pork products are also forbidden, as the pig is not considered a "clean" animal.

Fasting is also part of the discipline imposed by the faith. The word breakfast reminds us that, after a night

A man waits for day's end.

without food or drink, we break our fast in the morning. All over the Islamic world, Ramadan is the holy month of fasting. No food or water is permitted from sunrise to sunset. The fast is broken after evening prayers are completed, when the family comes together for a large meal. Non-Muslim visitors to Libya are obliged to respect the fast during Ramadan.

LANGUAGE

THE LANGUAGE THAT ORIGINATED among the Arabs of the Arabian peninsula is now spoken by some 150 million people around the world, from Morocco to Malaysia. It is the official language of Libya.

ARABIC

Arabic belongs to the Afro-Asiatic family of languages and is further classified as a Semitic language. Semites are people from the Middle East who are believed to have descended from Shem, Noah's eldest son. The Semitic languages are spoken in North Africa and the Middle East. They include Hebrew and Amharic. Modern spoken Arabic has regional differences, but most Arabic-speaking countries use standard Arabic, based on the language of the Koran, in their books and newspapers.

ANCIENT AFRICA

The most ancient language of Libya is the Numidian language of the Berbers that is still spoken in isolated places in Jabal Nafusah. A modified form of this language remains in *tifinagh* (tee-fee-nawkh), the geometrical alphabet used by the Tuareg. Most Libyan Berbers have adopted Arabic.

Opposite: **Libyans in Ghadamis read the Koran.**

Below: **Libyans use Arabic at work.**

91

In chess, a game adopted by Christian Europe from the Islamic world, several of the terms we use today come from the Arabic or Persian languages. The word checkmate comes from *shah mat*, meaning the king is dead. The castle is also called the rook, which comes from the Persian *rukh* (like the huge "roc" that swooped down upon Sinbad in the *Arabian Nights* story). The word rook can also mean chariot; the castle/rook moves in a similar straight and powerful manner. The bishop in Arabic is called *al-Fil*, the elephant.

Above: **Arabic words are everywhere in Libya.**

Opposite: **Arabic script on the side of a fountain in the courtyard of the Tripoli Castle.**

ARABIC WORDS

In the years when Muslim traders sailed to the shores of the Mediterranean, many European languages adopted words from Arabic. Many places in Arab countries have Arabic names beginning with "Al."

English words such as alcohol, almanac, alfalfa, alcove, and algebra come from Arabic. Here are some others: admiral, coffee, giraffe, caravan, lemon, kebab, and marzipan.

Words with connected meanings in Arabic often contain the same pattern of consonants. For example, s-l-m is the root of such words as *salaam* (meaning peace), Islam, and Muslim.

ARABIC AND THE KORAN

Among the earliest teachings of Islam was the necessity for Muslims to be taught to read. Only then could they read the Koran.

As all Muslims are required to study the Koran, all Muslims must learn Arabic, because the Koran must be read in Arabic. Muslims believe that the Koran would not truly reflect the word of God in any other language. That is why Arabic is the official spoken and written language of Libya. But because there are many specialists from the Western world working in Libya, other languages such as English and Italian are spoken by some.

The word Allah is constantly on the lips of Muslims. It is considered polite to refer to Allah often in conversation. "Praise Allah," "By Allah's permission," and "Allah is great" are as common in conversation as "Goodbye." Even so simple a matter as agreeing to meet a friend at a certain time will be guarded by the phrase "insh-allah," or if Allah wills it.

VISUAL BEAUTY

Arabic was originally written in brush strokes, and its letters still look as if they have been painted rather than printed. The early editions of the Koran were hand-written and are beautiful to look at. Calligraphers used to be held in high regard, largely because there was no printing in the Islamic world until the 18th century.

Muslims are forbidden to depict God in pictures, but they love to describe him in picturesque words. So Arabic calligraphy is one of their primary art forms. In the past, as most calligraphers and their readers knew the Koran by heart, beautiful lettering became more important than legibility.

ARABIC NUMERALS

The number system used for centuries by the Christian world was invented by the Romans and is still known as Roman numerals. In this system, different letters stand for numbers. *C* stands for a hundred and *M* for a thousand, because they are the first letters of the Latin words *centum* and *mille*. So for the number two thousand, two hundred, and twenty-two, the Romans wrote MMCCXXII.

How much simpler it is for people today to write 2,222. Although each figure 2 looks the same, it stands for a different amount according to its position in the number. That is because we use Arabic numerals. This number system was introduced to Spain at the end of the 10th century by the Arabs, who probably borrowed the system from India about 200 years earlier.

It took another 500 years for the rest of Europe to accept this new system. Thanks to the Arabs, the European world was introduced to the use of the digit 0. Without this symbol, the invention of decimals would have been impossible.

Interestingly, it was Caliph

Customers bargain over price with a salesman in a Tripoli souk.

Haroun al-Raschid (made famous in the *Arabian Nights* stories, though he was a very real person) who did much to spread mathematical ideas. He had many old Greek books translated into Arabic, including Euclid's *Elements* on mathematics in 1482.

Arabs were also skilled astronomers. Astronomical terms such as zenith and nadir come from Arabic. Arabs knew enough of astronomy and geography to calculate the circumference and diameter of the earth. After all, it was from "the East" (perhaps Persia and the Arabian Desert) that the Three Wise Men followed the star to Bethlehem.

PROBLEMS WITH POPULAR LITERATURE

The Koran is written in classical Arabic, an old-fashioned form of the language. Classical Arabic is used in nearly all written and printed material in Arab countries, but it is not the way the people speak.

In fact, the Libyan dialect is considerably different. As a result, the Arabic that children speak is different from the Arabic they have to read. That means there are very few books for children. The few available ones that have been written in beautiful classical Arabic are too difficult to be understood by children. Thus, there is very little popular reading material.

However, Libyan publishers are now working to produce better books for children, and in recent years the quality and quantity of available publications has increased.

Some of the literature available in Libya.

A customer in conversation with a store clerk. Rituals of communication are taken very seriously in Libya.

SPELLING ARABIC IN ENGLISH

Writing Arabic words with the English alphabet poses constant problems because there are many sounds in Arabic for which our alphabet has no equivalent. Even so famous an Arab name as Muhammad can also be spelled Mohammed, Mehmet, and Mahomet. Yet none of these gives the exact sound of the true Arabic pronunciation.

In this book, the spellings preferred by English-speaking Muslims have been used. There are books in which Muslim is Moslem, and Koran is Al-Qur'an.

IN CONVERSATION

Muslims constantly encounter the ancient Arabic language in their daily prayers, the reading of the Koran, and in Arabic writings. God is constantly invoked in conversation, and sayings such as "in the name of God," "thanks be to God," and "may God be with you" are constantly on the believer's lips. *Insh-allah*, meaning if God wills it, is used in various situations, from a polite refusal to sealing an agreement.

Traditional manners require a series of questions, each with its proper answer, when inquiring about another's health and family. Hands are clasped until the ritual questions have been answered. Important conversations are always accompanied by coffee. It would be the height of bad manners to begin a serious discussion before the pot was finished.

Libyans, anxious not to offend the authorities, may appear humorless, and they are careful never to be seen laughing at anyone. But they do have a sense of humor which is often African in flavor. .

The normal Libyan greeting is *Salaam aleikum* (peace be with you), to which the correct reply is *Aleikum as-salaam* (and also with you). Another normal greeting is *Sabbahakum Allah bi'l-khair* (Allah give you a good morning). Among the Tuareg, a normal greeting includes letting one's palm slide gently across the other's and then pulling the hand back to touch the chest.

In Libya it is extremely rude to criticize someone to his or her face, so when disagreements occur, family and friends are often brought in to mediate. Tradition demands courtesy in public, and family matters are considered strictly private. Women are never discussed in public, especially not by name. Women may discuss the men in their friends' families, but among men, it is considered immodest and vulgar to mention the women in a man's family.

Gestures form a significant part of any good conversation. The tips of four fingers joined to the thumb is a gesture used to emphasize anything. "No" is often accompanied with a click of the tongue and a toss of the head.

Camel herders taking a break and sharing a conversation.

97

IN THE MEDIA

All forms of public entertainment in Libya are restricted to the accepted agenda prescribed by Islam. All expressions of Western culture, including books, films, magazines, posters, and Christian institutions, are forbidden or viewed with disapproval. Ever since Arabic became the official language in 1969, all street signs, advertisements, and shop names must be written in Arabic. Speaking languages such as English and Italian in public is discouraged.

Radios and television sets are easy to purchase in Libya, and most families own one or the other. The state both owns and controls the media, and the censors are quick to edit or cut programs that they see as threatening moral values, demeaning Libya, or glorifying the West. The government runs Libya's two radio stations: the Great Socialist People's Libyan Arab Jamahiriya Radio, which broadcasts in Libya only in Arabic, and the Voice of Africa, an external station that also runs programs in English and French.

When Libya's national television station was launched in 1968, it was the only channel available in the country. With the advent of satellite technology, however, those who can afford it enjoy wider access to international programming. Stations that broadcast in Arabic, such as the news channel Al-Jazeera and the Egyptian-run NileTV, which even has an Arabic version of Sesame Street, remain popular. The Great Socialist People's Libyan Arab Jamahiriya Television is still state-run and broadcasts a mix of Libyan propaganda and entertainment programs from around the Arab world. During the month of Ramadan, popular soap operas made in Egypt entertain the population and are often a chief topic of conversation. Cinemas in Libya show imported films produced in Arab countries. Movies are also carefully censored before screening.

The Libyan government has a monopoly on the distribution of books. This means that they buy books for distribution to schools and libraries only after examining and approving them. The time this takes is not encouraging for publishers or authors. If an author expresses opinions that the government book selectors disagree with, the book will not be bought at all.

Freedom of the press is guaranteed "within the principles of the revolution." But no published writing that criticizes the revolution or says anything offensive against Islam is allowed.

Foreign journalists known to have criticized Libya are forbidden to enter the country. Foreign newspapers and

The pilot's instructions in the Libyan Arab Airlines are in Arabic.

magazines must be approved by the censors before they are sold in Libya, and they are often a few days late by the time they appear in newsstands. Libya's daily newspaper *Al-Fajr al-Jadid* (*The New Dawn*) has both an Arabic and an English edition, and three other newspapers are also published regularly. The newspapers are all subject to intense censorship.

Apart from religious texts, novels and poetry collections are also read, all in Arabic and with a strong pro-Libyan message, in contrast to the poor image of the Arab in general and the Libyan in particular that is conveyed by Western literature. Qadhafi's three-volume *Green Book* has a fair claim to being the most widely read publication in Libya after the Koran.

ARTS

LIBYAN CULTURE is almost totally dependent on Islamic arts and traditions. In all visual arts Islam does not allow any representation of living things. Muslims believe that anything created by God is perfect and that it would be wrong to copy the sublime in an imperfect way, so there can be no human figures in pictures, sculpture, decorations, or designs. To make a carving or painting of a human being that can be admired would be like making an idol to be worshiped. Instead, Libyan artists and architects use intricate patterns of geometric designs or flowers.

CAVE PAINTINGS

The oldest form of art in Libya is rock paintings. In Fezzan, an Italian expedition found a series of rock paintings that are more than 5,000 years old. Some are painted solid red or black, others in a scraped style resembling rock engraving.

Although less spectacular, the rock paintings must have a similar origin to the rock art discovered in Algeria's Tassili N'ajjer, which is located near the Libyan border. The oldest rock paintings depict the Sahara as a green pasture with people hunting elephants, antelopes, and giraffes. The whole history of the Sahara is portrayed in the paintings at Tassili N'ajjer. After the hunters came cattle herders such as the Fulani in Nigeria. Then came paintings of chariots and horses, almost Cretan in style. Lastly, dated to about 100 B.C., there are pictures of people and camels, a clear indication of the changing geography of the Sahara.

Opposite: **A Libyan crafts-man engraving a copper plate.**

Below: **The unique Serpent Fountain, built by Turks.**

Above: **A beautiful wedding necklace and accompanying dress.**

Opposite: **Carpets gracing the interior of a Ghadamis mosque.**

AN INSTINCT FOR ORNAMENT

Examining Islamic art, one becomes convinced that Muslim artists hated blank space. But they never made "art for art's sake." Decoration was used to beautify everyday life, so carpets, pottery, windows, fountains, and houses became canvasses for Muslim artists.

Libyan craftwork used to include inlaid metalwork, pottery with the glazed tiles called faience, leatherwork, weaving, and embroidery. However, many craft shops have disappeared since Qadhafi encouraged nationalized production. Traditional Berber designs feature zigzags and triangles, often in earthy colors of rusty brown and dark blue. Arab patterns use more flowing, floral shapes known as arabesques.

THEMES

Islamic tradition has favored abstract patterns and elaborate scrollwork, often starkly geometric against a dark background. The polygon is the most common shape. It is easy to see that Muslim artists admired bees with their hexagonal cells for honey, and spiders with star-shaped, concentric webs. Flowers are popular too, often portrayed as circles or decorated segments.

CARPETS

The origin of the knotted pile rug is lost in time, but certainly the method was invented somewhere in the Middle East, quite possibly in Turkey. It seems likely that these precious and artistic possessions were originally designed as wall hangings rather than rugs to be used underfoot.

The skill of carpet weaving probably came to Libya with the arrival of Islam. And while locally made rugs are still found in Libya, the best ones

are imported. The coastal city of Misratah is noted for its carpet industry. Carpet weaving has been called the highest form of art in Islam. Carpets mass-produced in Libya today bear little resemblance to the traditional masterpieces that could take a whole family as long as a year to weave.

The most common form of carpet is the prayer rug, used by Muslims during worship. The arched design imitates the *mihrab* in the mosque that points in the direction of Mecca, which the worshiper must face. A Muslim will unroll a prayer rug in the street or in the desert rather than pray on "unclean" ground.

The design, following Islamic custom, features flowers or geometric patterns. Opinions differ on whether these designs were inspired by a love of gardens or whether the carpets inside the home compensated for the lack of flowers outside.

MUSIC

Muhammad himself seemed to have disapproved of music, fearing perhaps that people might enjoy it too much and forget the seriousness of life. A sanctioned form of music is the chanting of the Koran by a special chanter known for his voice. Koranic chanting is melodious and strikingly beautiful, unaccompanied by musical instruments.

Nevertheless, Arab culture finds ways to incorporate music into daily life, and songs and music celebrate special occasions such as feasts and holidays. Arab singers are renowned for their performing abilities and love songs, which are often taken from traditional Bedouin poetry.

Considering its desert origins, it is not surprising to find that Arab music relies on the voice rather than on musical instruments, although the lyre, cane pipe, drum, and tambourine accompany the singers' voices. The drum is a major component of Arab music. People like to dance to the music, although men and women are segregated when they dance.

Libyan musicians playing traditional musical instruments.

The old poet-singers of the Bedouin sang songs about great deeds or popular heroes, much like the wandering minstrels of medieval Europe. The words were more important than the tune. The *huda* song of the camel drivers has a rhythm that is supposed to echo the movement of the camel's feet.

Music in the Western world is based on a scale of eight notes, with half tones between five of them. Arabic music, on the other hand, has quarter tones as well—a variation that makes tunes sound mournful and exciting, exotic and beautiful.

ARCHITECTURE

An Arab city may seem like a maze of jumbled buildings, but much thought actually goes into its planning. The narrow alleyways provide vital shade, reduce dust, and save space. Privacy is essential—Islamic custom ensures that no door is directly opposite another, and window sills must be at least 5 feet 9 inches (1.7 m) above ground level. Streets may seem narrow, but they must be wide enough to allow two fully loaded camels to pass each other.

A visitor to Tripoli today will instantly see the contrast between the architect-designed, pastel-shaded villas of the rich suburbs and the shanty towns on the outskirts of the city. Stone-faced minarets rise above domed 18th-century mosques. Beside them are patterned gardens and courtyards. A block away will be the rubble of destroyed hovels or a high-rise apartment building. Traveling south, one sees houses and mosques built of sunbaked mud bricks. Square or with hand-smoothed pointed shapes, they are often whitewashed for a touch of coolness and durability.

The architectural design of the Assai Al Hamra is typical of many buildings in Libya.

The magnificent Roman ruins at Sabrata.

CLASSICAL RUINS

Sabrata, 40 miles (64 km) west of Tripoli, holds the remains of a splendid Roman theater that could seat 5,000 people under colonnades 80 feet (24 m) high. At the front of the stage is a marble relief showing the entertainment delights of drama, comedy, dance, and music. The area that was the marketplace had shops with solid stone counters where olives and olive oil, fruit and grain, hides and ivory, and live birds and slaves were sold to Rome.

Even more splendid was Leptis Magna. Once a Carthaginian settlement, it later became a Roman city of 80,000 people. It was brought to its final splendor by one of its own sons, the dark-skinned, black-bearded Emperor Septimius Severus. The magnificent public baths were erected under Emperor Hadrian.

Then there are the ruins of Cyrene, situated on a Cyrenaica hillside overlooking the sea. Although Greek in origin, the remains are far more Roman, including a forum, a theater, and baths.

KAIROUAN AND SILPHIUM

For the best examples of North African Islamic design, one must look farther west to Kairouan, once one of the holy cities of Islam in the days when the land was called Ifriqiya. The great mosque there is strictly practical, yet it is one of the most beautiful buildings. A single, huge square minaret acts as a landmark and a fortress gate through which grateful travelers can reach the sheltered enclosure inside (like the yard of the Arab caravanserai). The blank outside walls give no hint of the elegant, arcaded courtyard within. The mosque itself has simple round arches that link rows of sturdy columns with just a hint of floral decoration at their tops, giving the impression of an endless forest.

Another example of North African Islamic architecture is Cyrene, once the home of famed doctors and the long-vanished medicinal herb, silphium. Julius Caesar had 1,500 pounds (680 kg) of silphium stored away, but by the time Nero became emperor a hundred years later, only one plant could be found in Cyrene for him to use.

After the Arab invasions came the invasion of sand. Many of the marble columns of Leptis Magna were plundered by a French consul as a gift for King Louis XIV to help build Versailles. Then King George IV acquired what was left of them to make imitation ruins beside Victoria Water, an ornamental lake he had created. The bulk of the cities remained buried until the Italian invasion, when Benito Mussolini, eager to rediscover the greatness of Rome, had them excavated.

And yet the most exciting remains of Libya remain undiscovered. The ruins of Berber and Saharan towns still lie somewhere inland beneath sweeping sands. They will have to wait, because excavating teams from abroad are not welcomed by the Libyan authorities.

LEISURE

For many Libyans, especially those living in the open desert, leisure is constrained by the need to survive. In pastoral families, when children are old enough, they are expected to help with the household chores and with the herd or crops. Such serious demands leave little time for play.

LEISURE ATTRACTIONS

Libyans living in the cities have no clubs or bars in which to relax. After the revolution, Qadhafi shut down night entertainment spots, which encouraged a lifestyle contradicting strict Islamic law.

Nevertheless, there are avenues for recreation in Libya. People in the cities can watch a movie in a theater or meet friends at a café. Sports, especially soccer, are not only leisure pursuits but have become careers for professional athletes. Horse and camel racing are also popular in the country.

Libya has many museums, most of which exhibit archeological and Islamic artefacts. Examples are the Jamahiriya Museum of Archeology and Prehistory in the Tripoli Castle, and the Leptis Magna Museum at Al Khums, east of Tripoli.

Opposite: **Libyans taking a weekend stroll at an open-air market in Tripoli.**

Below: **Visitors enjoying the fine art in the Tripoli Museum.**

SPORTS

In the first years of independence, Libya hoped to show its sporting prowess in the international arena. Its Olympic debut was in 1968, when three competitors were sent to the Summer Games in Mexico City. They did not win any medals. After Qadhafi's coup in 1969, there was a very different attitude toward international relations.

At the Munich Olympics in 1972, Arab terrorists held several members of the Israeli team hostage and murdered 11 of them. Libya appeared to have been involved. The weapons used by the terrorists had been smuggled into Germany in Libyan diplomatic baggage. When Qadhafi hailed the five terrorists who were killed in the incident as martyr heroes, Libya was banned from participating in the Olympic Games. However, after UN sanctions were suspended in 1999, Libya took part in the Summer Games of 2000 and the Winter Games of 2002. Libya also has a team that participates in the international Special Olympic Games.

Libya's most popular sport is soccer. Matches between local teams are enthusiastically supported, and crowds often gather around a radio to listen to a broadcast. The Libyan Arab Jamahiriya Football Federation, founded in 1962, is a member of international soccer organizations.

HORSES

Horses have been a source of national pride since long before the Arabs arrived in North Africa. In 1229 B.C. an Egyptian Pharaoh's soldiers captured 14 chariots from a Libyan chief, which means that horses were being used in Libya over 3,000 years ago. We know that horse-drawn chariots were racing across the Sahara by 1000 B.C. According to the Bedouin, the Queen of Sheba gave magnificent Arab stallions to King Solomon. Such horses could easily have come to her kingdom from Africa, through the regular trade route across the Red Sea.

It was the ancestors of the Libyans who introduced the Greeks to four-horse chariot racing. That was also how the Romans caught on to the idea. The Greek historian Herodotus described, in about 470 B.C., how the Garamantes, warriors from Fezzan, chased Ethiopian cave dwellers in their four-horse chariots. The Roman Emperor Septimius Severus, from Libya's Leptis Magna, took Arab stallions to Britain as race horses.

Above: **Libyan horsemen, in full Bedouin attire, take part in a traditional horse race.**

Opposite: **Libya's soccer players represent the country in international tournaments.**

"I NAME THEE HORSE"

The Bedouin sing about the speed, loyalty, and beauty of Arabian horses in praise poetry. Here is a translated Bedouin praise poem:

When Allah willed
to create the horse,
He said to the South Wind,
"Of thy substance
shall I create a new being,
for the glory of my chosen people
and the shame of my enemies."

And the South Wind replied,
"Do thou so, Most Mighty."
Then Allah took to himself
a handful of wind,
and breathed upon it
and created a horse
of red-bay color like gold,
and he said, "I name thee horse."

MAD ABOUT HORSES   Libyans are mad about horses. There are frequently official and unofficial horse races. And the racing camel, the *mehari* (meh-HAH-ree) is also a mean contender.

The Arabian horse is recognized as the oldest breed in the world. However, it is not certain if it originated in Arabia as its name suggests. After Muhammad was defeated in a battle in A.D. 625 because of a lack of horses, he encouraged horse breeding as a pious and religious duty.

To make sure that horses remained of totally pure pedigree, a horse's ancestry was considered sacred. If horses were captured during the constant raiding, the Arabs promptly set about checking on the pedigree of any captured mare. A messenger would be sent to the defeated ones to determine this information. And the information would be given, even if there was a storm of protest at the theft of so wondrous a horse.

Pure-breed horses were so important that in later years, Muslims were forbidden to sell Arabian horses to Christians so that the stock would remain a unique cultural treasure. Today, pure Arabian horses are some of the most distinguished breeds in the world and often win prizes at international competitions.

Tuareg riders taking part in a ceremony in the Sahara Desert.

A troop of Libyan Girl Guides called Buds.

SCOUTS AND GIRL GUIDES

Scouting activities have spread fast in Libya since their introduction in 1954, even though Qadhafi at one point accused the Boy Scouts of America of being a front for the Central Intelligence Agency. Scouts and Guides in Libya are particularly active in the field of environmental conservation, tree-planting, and building farm roads. They also help the elderly and the handicapped, visit hospitals, and undergo first-aid training. They provide more service to their own community than do Scouts and Guides in some other parts of the world.

And, of course, they go camping. There are national Jamborees every few years, and they take part in joint activities with Scouts and Guides from other African countries. Libyan Scouts and Guides may also go to their meetings in the desert riding camels.

The Libyan Scout's "promise and law" are much the same as for other Scouting associations worldwide. Their motto is *Wa A'eddou* (Be Prepared).

113

TRADITIONAL GAMES

The Bedouin play a game that uses an eight-by-six grid of small holes in the sand. Players in turn place a pebble or bean into a hole and try to get three in a straight line. Each time a player succeeds, he or she removes one of the opponent's pebbles. There is also the game of *isseren* (IS-ser-en), which is played by throwing six split sticks into the air and scored by counting how many fall with the split side up. Chess and dominoes are also played.

TOURISM AND TRAVEL

During the 1990s tourism in Libya was nearly nonexistent because of sanctions that prohibited civilian air travel to and from Libya. Since UN sanctions were suspended in 1999, tourism in Libya has become a growing industry. Well-preserved Roman ruins at Leptis Magna and the ancient Greek city of Cyrene attract visitors from all over the world.

Nevertheless, it remains difficult to obtain visas to visit Libya. Would-be tourists must have Arabic translations of all their personal details in their passport before any Libyan People's Bureau (as Libyan embassies are called) will begin to process the visa application. All nationalities are welcome, but people who have previously visited Israel are forbidden to enter the country. Airport searches are very strict. Anything considered anti-Libya or harmful to Islamic morality (such as pork, alcohol, and pornography) is forbidden, as is anything made in Israel.

Under sanctions, Malta and other countries in the Arab world signed treaties of cooperation with Libya and allowed citizens to enter and travel freely in both countries. Overland trips to neighboring Tunisia and Egypt by bus, and to Malta by boat, were very popular.

The Mehari, one of the better hotels in the country.

After 1999 the number of Libyans traveling abroad increased dramatically, and now they can travel everywhere except the United States. Popular vacation destinations include Egypt, Tunisia, Saudi Arabia, Syria, and Malaysia. Few Libyans travel to Western countries, either because they cannot afford it or because they do not feel welcome.

Libya has had a difficult history of dealing with foreign workers, who are often blamed for corrupting the country's morals and encouraging crime. In 1985 Libya expelled about 40,000 Tunisian workers, along with thousands from Mali, Mauritania, Niger, and Syria.

Today, Libyans can travel easily around Africa and the Arab world, but Western governments require strict background checks for Libyans entering their countries. The longed-for hajj to Mecca is easy to manage, now that international flights are allowed from Libya's two international airports.

FESTIVALS

LIBYA HAS TWO KINDS OF NATIONAL HOLIDAYS: political and religious. Although the political celebrations take place on fixed days of the year as in the Western world, the religious festivals are part of the Islamic lunar calendar, which means they occur 10 to 12 days earlier every year.

Opposite: **A horse racing festival in Libya.**

Below: **Children parading a flag during National Day at the Green Square.**

NATIONAL HOLIDAYS

National Day, the anniversary of the revolution, is on September 1 and is marked with speeches and parades to celebrate the start of the Jamahiriya regime. The other main national holiday is Independence Day on December 24. It celebrates the original granting of independence to the country in 1951.

Libya also celebrates national holidays on March 2 (Declaration of People's Authority), June 11 (Evacuation Day), and October 7 (Italian Evacuation Day).

On Evacuation Day on June 11, Libyans not only celebrate the day when U.S. forces left in 1970, but also commemorate the U.S. bombing of Tripoli by tying black scarves around their heads.

117

THE MAJOR ISLAMIC FESTIVALS:

Day of Hijrah	Islamic New Year
Tenth Muharram	Fast Day
Milad un-Nabi	Birthday of Prophet Muhammad
Lailat al-Mi'raj	Night of Ascension
Lailat al-Bara'ah	Night of Forgiveness
Ramadan	Month of Fasting
Lailat al-Qadr	Night of Power
Id al-Fitr	End of Ramadan
Id al-Adha	Feast of Sacrifice

LUNAR CALENDAR

Just like many other Islamic countries in North Africa and the Middle East, Libya follows the Islamic calendar. This means that Islamic years are dated from A.D. 622—the year of Muhammad's departure from Mecca to Medina. Months are known as lunar months, each beginning with the new moon. Consequently, the Islamic year is about 10 days shorter than the Western year. Islamic festivals can take place in different seasons of the year because they are held 10 to 12 days earlier than in the previous year.

ISLAMIC FESTIVALS

DAY OF HIJRAH (ISLAMIC NEW YEAR) When Muhammad began preaching in Mecca, there was a plot to kill him by the merchants in Mecca who feared they would lose money if too many people followed Muhammad's teachings. With the help of friends, Muhammad escaped into the desert and hurried north to Medina, where he knew he would be welcomed. As this was the beginning of the first Islamic community, it is counted as the first day of the first Islamic year. It was later decided that the first day of the month of Muharram (moo-HAR-ram) should be the beginning of the Islamic year. Hijrah Day is a time when Muslims remind themselves of the stories of Muhammad and his early companions, and they send greetings to their friends.

TENTH MUHARRAM Also known as Ashura (a-SHOO-ra), this is a day of fasting to remember Moses' success in leading the Israelites out of slavery in Egypt. Tenth Muharram is also the day Muhammad himself kept a fast and instructed that others do the same. No weddings or public entertainment take place on this day.

MILAD UN-NABI Milad un-Nabi (mee-LAD an-na-BEE), or the birthday of Prophet Muhammad, is celebrated throughout the Islamic world. On this occasion, the birth, life, and teachings of Muhammad are recounted in readings and prayers. Libyan children usually set off firecrackers, and the evening meal includes every possible variety of dried fruit. Often, the whole month of Rabi ul-Awwal, which is the third month in the Islamic calendar, is spent celebrating Muhammad's birth and life.

Traditional Libyan musicians performing at a festival.

LAILAT AL-MI'RAJ Lailat al-Mi'raj (LAY-lat ul-MIK-raj) is the 27th day of the month of Rajab (re-JAB). On this day, Muslims celebrate Muhammad's night journey from Mecca to the rock in Jerusalem. From there, according to legend, he visited heaven on the back of his horse, Al Buraq. The bare rock forms the center of the beautiful Dome of the Rock mosque in Jerusalem, and is also believed to be the Altar of Sacrifice of Solomon's Temple. There are channels cut in the rock to carry away the blood of animal sacrifices.

During festivals, children look forward to visiting carnivals, where they can ride a Ferris wheel.

LAILAT AL-BARA'AH The night of the full moon, Lailat al-Bara'ah (LAY-at ul-BAR-ah), is two weeks before the start of Ramadan. On this Night of Forgiveness, Muslims prepare for Ramadan by seeking forgiveness for old grievances against one another. Special prayers are offered, for it is believed that this night will decide a person's destiny for the coming year.

RAMADAN The month of fasting is signaled by the sighting of the new moon. All healthy adults are bound to fast through the month of Ramadan. Fasting requires abstaining from food, drink, smoking, and sex between sunrise and sunset.

Visitors to Libya during Ramadan will find themselves forced to observe the fast, whether they are Muslim or not. If they do fast all day, what they will need most at sundown is water. That is why the first meal after nightfall is often a thick, spicy soup, fruit juice, and dates.

Depending on how rich a Libyan family is, there may be more food to follow. As the family eats, they will talk and laugh and play music. In fact, nights can get rowdy. Café nightlife can go on into the early hours of the morning. Ramadan is a time of joy as well as tribulation.

It is during Ramadan that Lailat al-Qadr (LAY-lat ul-KAHD-er), or the Night of Power, is celebrated with readings from the Koran and special prayers. The mosque is full of worshipers on this day. It commemorates the occasion when the angel Gabriel revealed the Koran to Muhammad for the first time.

As the month of Ramadan draws to a close, Muslims gather to watch for the new moon. When that appears, there is great rejoicing, for the festival of Id al-Fitr (Id ul-FIT-r) can begin.

ID AL-FITR After a month of fasting, this day of festivity is greeted with joy. The beginning of the day is greeted with *Id mubarak*, meaning happy feast. It is a time for a bath and new clothes, as a reminder that this should be a new beginning in peace and forgiveness. The house is specially decorated. Cards and presents are exchanged and money is given to the poor. Spicy pastries called *samosas* (sah-MOH-sahs) are usually served, along with a variety of sweet cakes and cookies filled with nuts, cream, and dates.

ID AL-ADHA The Feast of Sacrifice, or Id al-Adha (Id ul-a-DAH), is the climax of the hajj to Mecca. It commemorates the day when God stopped Abraham, called Ibrahim in the Islamic tradition, from sacrificing his son in obedience to God. Although the festival is mainly for those who have made the pilgrimage to Mecca, it is greeted with four days of rejoicing by all Muslims all over the world.

In memory of the sacrifice, it is customary for Muslim families to sacrifice a sheep on the morning of the feast day and distribute the meat to the poor. This is the time for the whole family to be together. Guests are usually invited to dinner, and greetings are sent to family and friends.

FOOD

LIBYA IS ONE OF THE WEALTHIEST countries in Africa, but its population is growing far faster than its food supply. The diet of the average Libyan is unbalanced and lacks protein and essential vitamins.

FOOD SUPPLY

Libyans eat large quantities of bread and pasta, usually with a hot peppery sauce, but little meat, fresh fruit, or eggs. In the coastal regions along the Mediterranean, fruit, vegetables, wheat, and barley are grown, but these have to be supplemented by imported foods.

Libya's waters are rich with tuna, sardines, and other fish, but most of the fishing is done by Maltese, Greeks, and Italians. The local catch is not enough to meet the domestic demand, so thousands of tons of fish have to be imported every year.

One of Qadhafi's early policies discouraged small traders and replaced them with large supermarkets run by the state. The quaint Arab market, or souk, with its coffee shops and spice sellers alongside craft and leather stalls, rapidly disappeared. This policy has been changed and local produce is being encouraged once more.

Opposite: **A fruit and vegetable seller sets up his stall.**

Below: **A grocery store in Banghazi.**

FORBIDDEN FOODS

Muslims all over the world have strict laws about what they may eat and drink. Alcohol is forbidden, as is pork or any food cooked in pork fat. Animals must be killed in a certain way in order for the meat to be considered *halal*, or allowed. The butcher must say a prayer three times before he kills the animal and must kill it in as humane a way as possible.

EATING CUSTOMS

Although many Western-style fast-food eating places are beginning to appear in Libya, at home Libyans eat their meals in a way that originates in Islamic custom. Before and after a meal, they say prayers. Perfumed water may be passed around. In silence, each person dips three fingers into the bowl for a ceremonial cleansing.

Before the food is served, a round of bread is placed on each plate. Food is eaten with the fingers. It is the custom for the guest to start eating first; otherwise the eldest in the family will begin. It is not usual for Libyans to talk much at meal times.

After the meal, the hands are washed with warm water, and a prayer of thanks said.

Vegetable farmers in the Tripoli area.

BEDOUIN MANNERS

A visitor will be served ground coffee or mint tea, followed perhaps by a plate of dates, before any serious conversation starts. Many families in Libya still eat in the traditional manner. The men usually eat first, while the women wait out of sight once they have served the food. The dishes are placed in the center, with the guests sitting around. No cutlery is used. Only the right hand is used because to use the left hand is considered impure.

To welcome a guest with a proper feast is a delight for the desert Bedouin. Hospitality is a strong part of Islamic custom. Even when times are difficult, a family will prepare special dishes for the guest and make sure that there is plenty of meat—an expensive commodity in Libya. The show of hospitality is a reflection on the status of the family as much as on the guests themselves.

RAMADAN NIGHTS

Even though it is spent fasting, the month of Ramadan is a month of special food and drink enjoyed after sundown. *Iftar* (if-TAAr), or the breaking of the fast, is a very important time for the family to be together. Usually, the women of the household spend all day cooking for the evening meal. Dates, a hot lentil soup, and tamarind juice traditionally begin the meal, but after a brief wait, larger and more substantial dishes follow.

Salads and dips of lentils and beans, sizzling grilled meats, spicy rice or couscous, and plenty of hot, flat bread are an essential part of a late-night Ramadan meal. Food is often cooked in abundance so that there is plenty for guests, family, and friends. Desserts and pastries are of special importance during the holy month, when friends and relatives stop by. It would be unthinkable not to have a plate of pastries to offer visitors along with the obligatory tea and coffee. Popular pastries include *baklava* (bak-LA-va), a pistachio and honey pastry with crunchy layers, *basbousa* (bas-BOO-sa), a semolina cake soaked in flavored syrup, and *konafa bil ishta* (ko-NAA-fa bill ish-ta), a layered pastry filled with a sweet cream center. Although the pastries can be made at home, the more popular option is to buy huge plates from the local confectioner and bring them home in parcels tied with ribbon.

During the month of Ramadan, Libyans wake up before dawn to have the last meal before sunrise, called *suhur* (su-HUUR). To wake people, a musician often walks through the neighborhood streets banging a small drum. *Suhur* is not obligatory for fasting Muslims, but it is a popular option for people who find that they work better on a full stomach. The meal is often a light fruit juice, some rice or pudding, or salad and bread. Because it is at least an hour before sunrise, most people go back to sleep until morning, so the food must be light and easy to digest. Ramadan is a month of different schedules and routines, but a time of joy and togetherness.

SPICES

Spices and herbs are essential to Arab cooking. The most common include salt, pepper, saffron, ginger, garlic, cinnamon, cumin, and coriander.

Salt is found in the Sahara Desert in deposits left by long-vanished seas. It is used as a flavoring agent, a preservative, and an antiseptic. Pepper, ground from the dried berries of the pepper vine, gives food a hot, sharp taste.

Saffron, the dried stigmas of a purple-flowered crocus, is used to flavor and color rice. It is the most expensive spice in the world. Ginger is a root that is usually dried and preserved in syrup. It gives a rich tang to meat and fruit. Garlic is a strong-smelling, medicinal herb of the onion family and is used to tenderize meat and flavor salads.

Cinnamon, a fragrant stick of bark, is ground and used as an ingredient in curry powder or in cakes and puddings. Cumin is a sharp-tasting, mildly hot seed that is used whole or powdered in curry. Coriander adds flavor and aroma to many dishes. The seed is used whole or powdered, and the leaves are added to chutneys and sauces.

Above: One of the Libyan herdsmen's favorite dishes is lamb stewed with dates plucked from palm trees.

Opposite: Drinking tea is a big part of Libyan culture.

BREAD AND MEAT

Only Europeans in Libya eat leavened bread made with yeast. Most Libyans eat Arab breads such as *kesrah* (KES-raw), a flat pancake made of plain flour without yeast.

Considering that Libyan herdsmen tend about 6 million sheep, it is hardly surprising that lamb is the most common meat. It can be grilled, baked, stewed with vegetables and dates, minced or used in meatballs, and cooked on skewers as kebabs. Spit-roasted baby lamb is a traditional feast among the Bedouin. One popular local dish is a thick soup made with lamb stock and contains vegetables, grains, spices, and small pieces of lamb.

Other popular dishes are *shakshouka* (shak-SHOOK-ah), chopped lamb in tomato sauce with an egg on top; *baba ghanouj* (bah-bah-ga-NOOJ), sesame seeds and eggplant made into a paste, and usually eaten with bread; and *moloukhiya* (moo-LOH-kee-ah), steamed vegetables with rice.

DRINKS

In a hot climate, liquid refreshment is essential. Although Libyans grow grapes, their religion forbids the drinking of wine. There are plenty of imported bottled drinks, variations on colas, and fizzy fruit juices. There is also a locally made bright-red sparkling drink called *bitter* (BIT-r) and several hot drinks prepared from ginger, cinnamon, or aniseed.

More popular are coffee and mint tea. Arabs tend to drink their coffee in small cups—thick, black, and very sweet. Mint tea is also found all over Libya as a refreshing hot (and sometimes cold) drink. Libyans are believed to drink more tea per person than people in any other country. The humblest Bedouin tent will have its copper pot brewing over coals, and hospitality demands that a visitor accept at least three glasses or cups of the fragrant, sweetened liquid.

Making tea is a time-honored ritual. The host throws a portion of green tea into a metal teapot and pours boiling water from a kettle, which may sit on its own little brazier. Sugar is added generously, followed by a bouquet of fresh mint. The lid of the teapot is closed, and conversation resumes. After the host has poured tea into his own glass, tasted and tested it, it may at last be offered to his guests and family.

LAMB STEW WITH COUSCOUS

Couscous is a staple food in North Africa. It is made from semolina grains and looks like rice. It is usually served with a topping of stew consisting of meat (usually lamb or mutton), vegetables, and chickpeas. This recipe serves four.

2 pounds (1 kg) stewing lamb, cubed
2 chopped onions
2 cups water
Salt and pepper
1 teaspoon paprika
1 bunch fresh chopped parsley or coriander

1 teaspoon ground ginger
8 ounces (250 g) each of raisins and pitted prunes, soaked overnight
16 ounces (500 g) precooked couscous
3–4 tablespoons olive oil

Put the cubed lamb, one chopped onion, and enough water to cover the meat in a large pot. Add salt and pepper to taste. Add the paprika, parsley or coriander, and ginger. Bring to a boil and cover. Lower heat and simmer for an hour. Add the other onion, and simmer for another 15 minutes. Add the raisins and prunes, and cook for another 10 minutes. Put the couscous in a bowl, and add water a little at a time. Using your fingers, rub the couscous to make sure the grains do not stick together. The couscous should be slightly soft but not lumpy. Mix in the olive oil. Put the couscous in a mesh sieve, and place it directly over the simmering stew, so that the steam rises and warms the couscous. Stir the couscous in the sieve until it is hot and fluffy. Serve hot with the stew.

BASBOUSA WITH ALMONDS

Basbousa, a sweet cake made with semolina and almonds, is a popular dessert in the Middle East. Yogurt is sometimes added to the mix, and cream spread on top of the basbousa just before serving. This recipe serves four.

3 cups water
2 cups sugar
1 teaspoon lemon juice
1 cup blanched whole almonds
$^2/_3$ cup butter
1 cup semolina
Whole almonds

In a large pot, boil the water, sugar, and lemon juice for a few minutes, stirring the mixture constantly until it becomes thick and syrupy. Remove the mixture from the heat. Chop the almonds into small pieces. In a pan, fry the almonds with the butter and semolina, stirring constantly until dark golden in color. Add the syrup, and cook over low heat for 5 minutes, or until the mixture resembles cookie dough. Take the pan off the stove. Cover and leave to cool for about 5 minutes. Butter an 8-by-8-inch (20-by-20-cm) cake tin, and pour in the slightly cooled mixture about 1 inch (2.5 cm) high. Using a buttered spatula, flatten the mixture. Cut into small squares, and put one blanched almond in the center of each piece. Cool completely and serve.

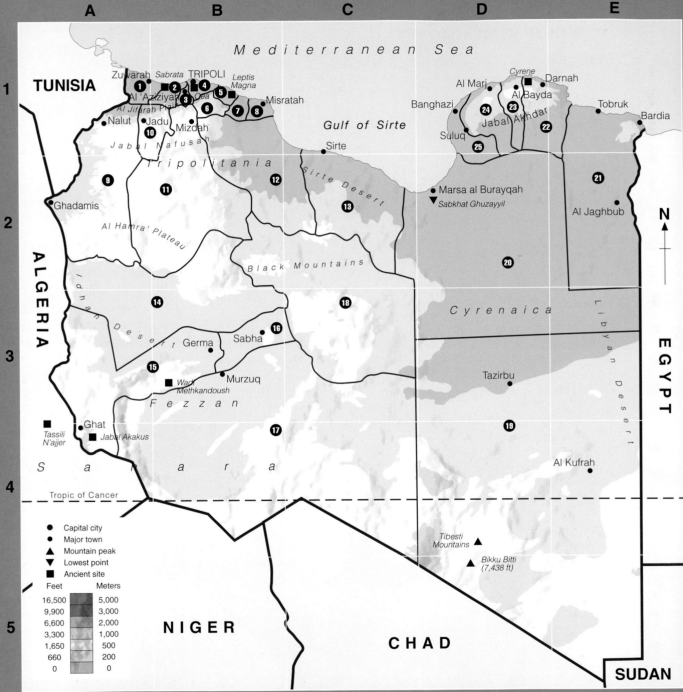

MAP OF LIBYA

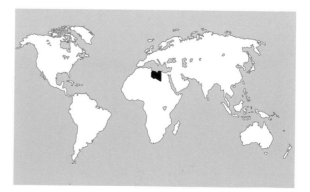

ECONOMIC LIBYA

Agriculture

- Barley
- Cattle
- Citrus Fruit
- Dates
- Olives
- Peanuts
- Soybeans
- Wheat

Services

- Airport
- Port

Natural Resources

- Natural Gas
- Oil

Development Project

- Great Man-Made River

Manufacturing

- Dairy Products
- Food Processing
- Furniture
- Oil Refining
- Textiles
- Water Bottling

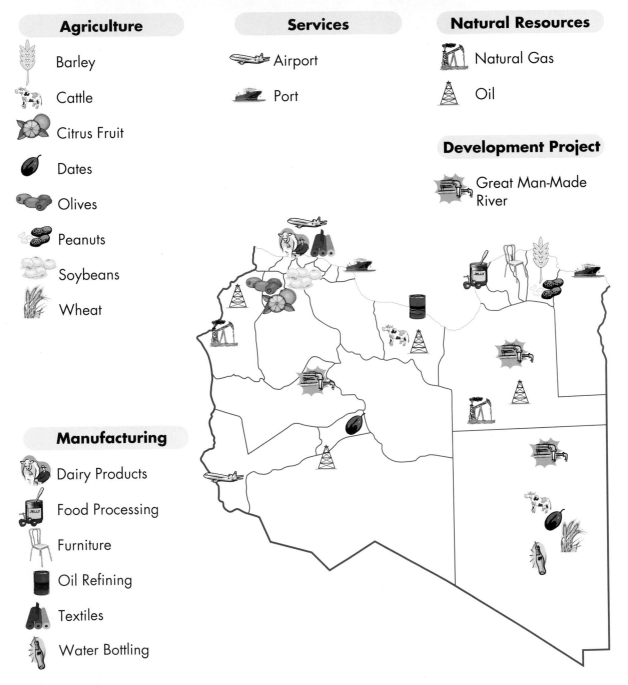

ABOUT THE ECONOMY

OVERVIEW

The Libyan economy is largely dependent on oil and petroleum, which make up the bulk of the country's exports. During the years of UN sanctions, Libya attempted to be as self-sufficient as possible. Over the past few years, increased international trade and foreign investment have allowed the country to specialize sectors such as petroleum production and crude oil export. Local production of food remains important on the country's agenda, and foreign-aid projects concentrate on increasing production. Tourism is also a growing sector in Libya, with many visitors from around the world traveling to see its ancient ruins and desert oases.

GROSS DOMESTIC PRODUCT (GDP)
US$41 billion (2002)

GDP PER CAPITA
US$7,600 (2002)

GDP SECTORS
Agriculture 9 percent, industry 45 percent, services 46 percent (2001)

CURRENCY
1 Libyan dinar (LYD) = 1,000 dirham
USD 1 = LYD 1.40 (September 2003)
Notes: 20, 10, 5, 1, $^{1}/_{2}$, $^{1}/_{4}$ dinar
Coins: 100, 20, 10, 5, 1 dirham

ECONOMIC GROWTH RATE
1.2 percent (2002)

LABOR FORCE
1.5 million (2000). Services 54 percent, industry 29 percent, agriculture 17 percent

UNEMPLOYMENT RATE
30 percent (2001)

IMPORTS
Tranportation equipment, machinery, food, manufactured goods

EXPORTS
Crude oil, refined petroleum products

MAIN TRADE PARTNERS
Italy, Germany, Spain, Turkey, France, Switzerland, Tunisia, United Kingdom, South Korea

OIL RESERVES
29.75 billion barrels (2002)

OIL PRODUCTION
1.5 million barrels a day (2003)

INDUSTRIES
Petroleum, food processing, textiles, cement, handicrafts

AGRICULTURAL PRODUCTS
Wheat, barley, olives, dates, citrus fruit, vegetables, peanuts, soybeans, cattle

CULTURAL LIBYA

Berber hilltop village
A former desert fortress, Jadu is still an active town and a center of Berber culture, where market days and traditional festivals are a bustle of colorful activity.

Tripoli
Highlights include the old walled city (medina), the Jamahiriya Museum with artifacts from Roman times, the arch in honor of Roman emperor Marcus Aurelius, souks, and the Red Castle (*Assai al-Hamra*).

Talmitha
Also known as Ptolemais, this coastal city was a Greco-Roman trading port and storage place for products on their way across the Mediterranean Sea. The ruins excavated here include palaces, fountains, and Roman baths and statues.

Greek ruins
Cyrene, an ancient Greek colony founded in 631 B.C. that later came under Roman rule, has the fountain and sanctuary of Apollo, a forum, a theater, baths, and a large second-century house.

Nalut
This town is famous for its Islamic architecture. The arches and passageways of the old bazaar and the central mosque, both more than 300 years old, are well-preserved.

Ghadamis
This oasis city, known as the pearl of the desert, is characterized by traditional desert architecture designed to provide cool relief from the desert heat.

Troglodyte dwellings
Until the last decade, the inhabitants of Gharyan lived in caves dug into the mountainside. These cave dwellings are still intact although the dwellers have moved to more modern housing.

Ancient rock art
The Akakus Mountains are home to prehistoric rock art that goes back 10,000 years, stunning rock formations, and caves. Among the rock carvings are those of giraffes, elephants, rhinoceroses, and crocodiles.

Garamantian Civilization
Many tombs, forts, water tunnels, and mud-brick buildings can be found at the site of the Garamantian Empire in Germa and Zinchecra, supposedly inhabited by a warlike people who were skilled chariot riders.

Leptis Magna
Widely regarded as the finest Roman ruins in North Africa, the monuments here include a piazza, elaborate arches, a circus, an amphitheater, a basilica, and the famous Hadrianic baths.

ABOUT
THE CULTURE

OFFICIAL NAME
Great Socialist People's Libyan Arab Jamahiriya

NATIONAL FLAG
Plain green. Green is the traditional color of Islam, which is the country's official religion.

NATIONAL SYMBOL
A black and gold eagle with a shield on its breast

POPULATION
5.5 million (2003)

POPULATION GROWTH RATE
2.4 percent (2003)

LITERACY
82.6 percent (2003)

CAPITAL
Tripoli

OTHER MAJOR CITIES
Banghazi, Tobruk, Sirte, Misratah, Zuwarah, Darnah, Sabha, Ghadamis

GOVERNMENT
Military dictatorship

OFFICIAL LANGUAGE
Arabic; English and Italian are also spoken.

LIFE EXPECTANCY
74 years for men, 78 years for women

GEOGRAPHICAL REGIONS
Tripolitania, Cyrenaica, Fezzan

RELIGION
Islam

ADMINISTRATIVE REGIONS
Ajdabiya, Al 'Aziziyah, Al Fatih, Al Jabal Al Akhdar, Al Jufrah, Al Khums, Al Kufrah, An Nuqat Al Khams, Ash Shati', Awbari, Az Zawiyah, Banghazi, Darnah, Ghadamis, Gharyan, Misratah, Murzuq, Sabha, Sawfajjin, Sirte, Tarabulus, Tarhunah, Tobruk, Yafran, Zlitan

ETHNIC GROUPS
Arabs, Berbers, Tuaregs, Italians, Greeks, Maltese, Egyptians, Pakistanis, Turks, Indians, Tunisians

LEADERS IN POLITICS
Muhammad Idris al-Sanusi—Libya's first and only king (1951–69)
Muammar Qadhafi—chairman of the Revolutionary Command Council and head of state since 1969

NATIONAL HOLIDAYS
National Day (September 1), Independence Day (December 24), Declaration of People's Authority (March 2), Evacuation Day (June 11)

TIME LINE

IN LIBYA	IN THE WORLD
8000 B.C.	
Herders and farmers live on the coastal plains of North Africa and the Mediterranean.	
3000 B.C.	
Berber groups begin to migrate into North Africa.	
1200 B.C.	**753 B.C.**
Phoenician sailors land on the Libyan coast.	Rome is founded.
700 B.C.	
Greeks begin to colonize the Libyan coast.	
146 B.C.	**116–17 B.C.**
The Romans destroy Carthage and occupy North Africa.	The Roman Empire reaches its greatest extent, under Emperor Trajan (98–17).
	A.D. 600
A.D. 642	Height of Mayan civilization
Umayyad general Amr Ibn Al-As conquers the Libyan coast for the Islamic empire.	
909	
Libya falls to the Fatimid dynasty.	**1000**
1510	The Chinese perfect gunpowder and begin to use it in warfare.
Spanish forces capture Tripoli.	**1530**
	Beginning of trans-Atlantic slave trade organized by the Portuguese in Africa.
1551	**1558–1603**
Ottoman armies reclaim Libya.	Reign of Elizabeth I of England
	1620
	Pilgrims sail the *Mayflower* to America.
	1776
	U.S. Declaration of Independence
	1789–1799
	The French Revolution
	1861
	The U.S. Civil War begins.
	1869
	The Suez Canal is opened.

IN LIBYA	IN THE WORLD
1911 Italians land on Tripoli.	
	1914 World War I begins.
	1939 World War II begins.
1940 Fighting during World War II begins in the deserts of Libya and Egypt.	**1945** The United States drops atomic bombs on Hiroshima and Nagasaki.
1951 The United Nations declares Libya an independent country; Muhammad Idris al-Sanusi becomes the first king.	**1949** The North Atlantic Treaty Organization (NATO) is formed.
1969 The September Revolution brings Colonel Muammar Qadhafi into power.	**1957** The Russians launch Sputnik. **1966–69** The Chinese Cultural Revolution
1980 Qadhafi announces the annexation of the Tibesti Mountains in Chad. French troops intervene and a long war begins.	
1988 Two Libyans are suspected of blowing up a plane over Lockerbie in Scotland.	**1986** Nuclear power disaster at Chernobyl in Ukraine
1989 Libya signs a peace treaty with Chad and withdraws from the Tibesti Mountains.	**1991** Break-up of the Soviet Union
1992 The United Nations imposes sanctions on Libya for harboring the Lockerbie suspects.	**1997** Hong Kong is returned to China.
1999 Libya agrees to hand over the Lockerbie suspects. The United Nations suspends sanctions but the U.S. trade embargo remains.	
2001 The Lockerbie trial ends. Diplomatic relations with Western governments improve.	**2001** Terrorists crash planes in New York, Washington, D.C., and Pennsylvania.
2003 The United Nations lifts sanctions on Libya.	**2003** War in Iraq

GLOSSARY

Amazigh
Another term for the Berbers, who are thought to be the indigenous people of North Africa.

bayt (bait)
An extended family unit.

Bedouin (BED-oo-in)
A desert nomad.

Carthage (KAR-thej)
An ancient civilization in North Africa.

Fezzan (fez-ZAN)
The inland desert of Libya.

ghibli (GIB-lee)
A sandstorm.

halal
Food that is allowed to be consumed by Muslims.

imam
The religious leader of a mosque.

kesrah (kes-RAW)
Libyan bread, made without yeast.

Kharijite (KAR-i-jait)
One of the sects of Islam.

Leptis Magna (lep-tis MAG-nah)
The ruins of an ancient Roman city in Libya located in Al Khums, to the east of Tripoli.

Maghreb
The Berber area of North Africa, normally including Morocco, Algeria, Libya, and Tunisia.

mehari (meh-HAH-ree)
A pedigree racing camel.

Oea (oh-EE-ah)
An ancient Roman city that occupied Tripoli's present-day location.

Phoenicians
The inhabitants of Phoenicia, an ancient region where present-day Lebanon is located.

Salaam Aleikum
A traditional Arab greeting that means "peace be with you."

sheikh
The head of an Arab village or camp.

souk
A covered market with many small shops.

Tassili N'ajjer (Tahs-sil-ee NAH-jer)
A mountainous area of the Sahara, in Algeria near Libya's southwestern border.

Tuareg (TWA-reg)
A nomadic desert people related to the Berbers.

wadi
A dry valley that sometimes forms an oasis.

FURTHER INFORMATION

BOOKS

Ahmen, Akbar. *Islam Today*. London: I. B. Tauris, 1998.

Gottfried, Ted. *Libya: Desert Land in Conflict*. Brookfield: Milbrook Press, 1994.

Harik, Ramsay and Elsa Marston. *Women in the Middle East: Tradition and Change*. Revised edition. London: Watts, 2003.

Harmon, Daniel. *Libya: Modern Middle East Nations and Their Strategic Place in the World*. Brookshire: Mason Crest Publishers, 2003.

Reese, Lyn. *Women in the Muslim World: Personalities and Perspectives from the Past*. New York: Women in World History Curriculum, 1998.

Robinson, Francis. *The Cambridge Illustrated History of the Islamic World*. Cambridge: Cambridge University Press, 1999.

Rogerson, Barnaby. *A Traveller's History of North Africa*. Cambridge: Interlink Publishing Group, 1998.

VIDEOS

Introduction to the Arab World. AMIDEAST, 1989.

Lost Treasures of the Ancient World 2: The Romans in North Africa. Kultur Video, 2000.

Young Voices from the Arab World: The Lives and Times of Five Teenagers. AMIDEAST, 1999.

WEBSITES

Arab.net: Libya. www.arab.net/libya

BBC News Country Profiles: Libya.
    http://news.bbc.co.uk/2/hi/middle_east/country_profiles/819291.stm

Imazighen in Libya. www.libyamazigh.org

Leptis Magna: Archeological and Historical Sites. www.leptismagna.com

Libya On Line Information and Entertainment at your fingertips. www.libyaonline.com

Libya: Our Home. http://ourworld.compuserve.com/homepages/dr_ibrahim_ighneiwa

Libyana: Culture of Libya. www.libyana.org

Libya Resources on the Internet. http://geocities.com/LibyaPage

Lonely Planet World Guide: Destination Libya.
    www.lonelyplanet.com/destinations/africa/libya

The Garamantes of the Fezzan. http://museums.ncl.ac.uk/garamantes/feztop.htm

The Sabr Foundation Islam 101. www.islam101.com

UN Security Council Global Policy Forum: Libya.
    www.globalpolicy.org/security/sanction/libya/indxirlb.htm

BIBLIOGRAPHY

Gottfried, Ted. *Libya: Desert Land in Conflict.* Brookfield: Millbrook Press, 1994.

Ham, Anthony. *Libya.* Lonely Planet Guides. London: Lonely Planet, 2002.

Metz, Helen Chapin. *Libya: A Country Study.* Washington, D.C.: U.S. Government Printing Office, 1990.

Simons, Geoff. *Libya: The Struggle for Survival.* New York: St. Martin's Press, 1993.

Tremlett, George. *Gadaffi: The Desert Mystic.* New York: Caroll & Graf Publishers, Inc., 1993.

Wright, John L. *Libya, Chad, and the Central Sahara.* Lanham, Maryland: Barnes & Noble, Inc., 1989.

Arab.net: Libya. www.arab.net/libya

BBC News Country Profiles: Libya.
    http://news.bbc.co.uk/2/hi/middle_east/country_profiles/819291.stm

Central Intelligence Agency World Factbook: Libya.
    www.cia.gov/cia/publications/factbook/geos/ly.html

Library of Congress Federal Research Division Country Studies: Libya.
    http://lcweb2.loc.gov/frd/cs/lytoc.html

INDEX